Aggregate and Industry-Level Productivity Analyses

STUDIES IN PRODUCTIVITY ANALYSIS
Volume II

AGGREGATE AND INDUSTRY-LEVEL PRODUCTIVITY ANALYSES

EDITED BY

Ali Dogramaci

Nabil R. Adam

Rutgers,
The State University
of New Jersey

Martinus Nijhoff Publishing
Boston/The Hague/London

Distributors for North America:
Martinus Nijhoff Publishing
Kluwer Boston, Inc.
160 Old Derby Street
Hingham, Massachusetts 02043

Distributors outside North America:
Kluwer Academic Publishers Group
Distribution Centre
P.O. Box 322
3300 AH Dordrecht, The Netherlands

Library of Congress Cataloging in Publication Data

Main entry under title:

Aggregate and industry-level productivity analyses.

  (Studies in productivity analysis; v. 2)
  Includes bibliographies and indexes.
  1. Industrial productivity—Addresses, essays,
lectures. 2. Industrial productivity—United States—
Addresses, essays, lectures. I. Dogramaci, A.
II. Adam, Nabil R. III. Series.
HC79.I52A34   338'.06'0973   80-18194

ISBN 0-89838-037-5

Printed in the United States of America

CONTENTS

ACKNOWLEDGMENTS

The editors and the contributing authors are deeply indebted to the referees for their invaluable comments and recommendations and for their numerous suggestions. We would like to express our deep personal appreciation for the thorough and constructive reviewing process provided by the referees whose names follow:

James W. Albrecht, Columbia University
Alice Amsden, Barnard College
Phoebus J. Dhrymes, Columbia University
Faye Duchan, Institute for Economic Studies
Len Foreman, New York Times, Inc.
Nelson M. Fraiman, International Paper Company
A. Gruen, Hunter College
Keith N. Johnson, Columbia University
Coskun Kulur, Istanbul Technical University
Daniel McFadden, University of California at Berkeley
Katherine Morgan, Montclair State College
J. C. Panayiotopoulos, Pireaus School of Graduate Studies
Kazuo Sato, State University of New York at Buffalo
Ronald Shephard, University of California at Berkeley

1 INTRODUCTION

Ali Dogramaci and Nabil R. Adam

1.1. OVERVIEW

With the decline of U.S. productivity growth, interest has surged to understand the behavior of productivity measures through time, the conceptual foundations of productivity analysis, and the linkage between productivity performance and other major forces in the economy. The purpose of this volume is to present a brief overview of some of the concepts used in aggregate and industry-level productivity analyses and the results of some of the recent research in this field.

The book is divided into three parts. Part I covers some of the methodological approaches used in aggregate and industry-level productivity studies. Part II deals with the movement of labor productivity measures through time. The papers in this part of the book study productivity changes as univariate time series and analyze some of the characteristics of the patterns displayed. The papers in Part III address the issues of measurement of capital, the relation of capital formation to productivity growth, and the relation of imported intermediate inputs to U.S. productivity performance.

1

1.2. THE ISSUES UNDER ANALYSIS

The concept of total factor productivity, which can be traced back to Tinbergen (1942) and Stigler (1947), was developed through time by the contributions of such researchers as Abramovitz (1956), Kendrick (1956), Solow (1957), Denison (1962), Griliches and Jorgenson (1966), and Jorgenson and Griliches (1967). It presently is used by a large number of researchers for macroeconomic as well as microeconomic productivity analysis.

The first paper in Part I presents a synthesis of concepts behind the measure of total factor productivity. In this paper, Ephraim F. Sudit and Nachum Finger discuss the production function theory in terms of its relation to total factor productivity measure. Within this context, the notions of separability assumption, the Divisia index, the translog production functions, issues related to measurement of output, and some of the concepts behind the measurement of capital are explained. For readers not acquainted with aggregate and industry-level approaches to productivity analysis, the chapter by Sudit and Finger will foster a better understanding of the later papers in this volume, especially Chapters 7 and 8 by John R. Norsworthy and Michael J. Harper, and Frank M. Gollop and Mark J. Roberts, respectively.

Part I also includes a chapter on the Leontief input-output approach to productivity analysis. In this chapter (Chapter 3), I. Douglas Moon presents a brief outline of the basic Leontief approach to productivity and follows it by a discussion of the dynamic aspects of interindustry relationships. The power of the Leontief approach to reflect the physical flows of goods and services between industries is especially appealing for researchers studying the impacts of technological changes that originate in certain industries and have an impact on others. Naturally the impacted industries can produce a response that leads to a feedback effect on the industries that originated the technological change; thus, one can think of many cycles of a dynamic process. The behavior of such relationships was modeled by Moon (1979) using a dynamic Leontief framework, and the stability properties of the system were investigated. The last segment of Chapter 3 briefly summarizes these findings and draws attention to the advantages of dynamic input-output models.

The remaining chapters in the book are empirical studies. In Part II, Chapter 4, Lawrence B. Cohen studies the behavior of indexes of output per man-hour through time and how the indexes of output and required production man-hours relate to each other over a span of about twenty years. He finds linear patterns that shift abruptly at certain points in time and discusses the implications for interpretation. This is followed by Salih N.

Neftci's study of U.S. labor productivity behavior during the business cycles. He develops a test for studying the possibility of asymmetry over the "ups" and "downs" of the business cycle using autoregressive representation and applies it to his data.

Part III begins with a paper by Tom Boucher who examines the economics of capital investment in the metalworking industries of the United States. By choosing a set of industries with a common technology, he is able to perform an examination of capital investment that takes into consideration quality changes occurring at the technology base. He concludes that changes in the quality of machinery, as measured by its output-producing capability, give insight to post–World War II productivity trends in these industries. The next paper, by Norsworthy and Harper, addresses the problem of measurement of capital at the aggregate level. It shows the importance of translog or Divisia aggregation of capital stock as compared to direct aggregations based on Cobb-Douglas functions. Having prepared more precise estimates on capital, Norsworthy and Harper move on to examine the effect of capital formation on labor productivity slowdown. They find no role for the period 1965–1973, but a significant role for the period 1973–1977. They also draw implications from the rising energy prices since 1973 that affected the substitution of capital for labor.

The final chapter of the book is concerned with the effects of rising prices of imported intermediate input to the U.S. economy. In this paper, Gollop and Roberts study individual industries within the context of translog production functions and find that increasing import prices have a detrimental effect on productivity growth rates. They also draw attention to the durable goods industries, which are especially affected by the process.

The papers presented in this book display differences in terms of choice of aggregation, methods for measurement of capital, treatment of intermediate inputs, temporal framework (in the sense of business-cycle fluctuations), and variations of production relations through time. These differences carry implications for future research. In addition, the reader should be aware of other approaches not covered in this volume, including those of Aigner and Schmidt (1980), Dogramaci (1981), Fuss and McFadden (1978), Gold (1977, 1979), and Kendrick and Vaccara (1980).

One of the possible objectives of future research is synthesis, or a constructive resolution of some of the present differences between existing methodologies. Understanding the present approaches, their implicit and explicit assumptions, and their differences is a prerequisite for approaching such an objective. The following seven chapters in this volume thus not only serve as original contributions on their own; they also serve as a group to illustrate to the reader subsets of common features and differences of metho-

4   ALI DOGRAMACI AND NABIL R. ADAM

dology that can then be studied with respect to other schools of thought. It is hoped that this opportunity for comparative study will lead to constructive further research.

REFERENCES

Abramovitz, M., 1956, "Resources and Output Trends in the United States since 1870," *American Economic Review* 46, no. 2:5–23.
Aigner, Dennis J., and Peter Schmidt, eds., 1980, "Specification and Estimation of Frontier Production, Profit and Cost Functions," Annals of Applied Econometrics, 1980-2, *Journal of Econometrics* 13.
Denison, Edward F., 1962, *Sources of Economic Growth in the U.S. and the Alternatives before Us,* Supplementary Paper 13, Washington, D.C.: Committee for Economic Development.
Dogramaci, Ali, ed., 1981, *Productivity Analysis: A Range of Perspectives,* Boston: Martinus Nijhoff Publishing.
Fuss, Melvyn, and Daniel McFadden, eds., 1978, *Production Economics: A Dual Approach to Theory and Applications,* vols. 1 and 2, Amsterdam: North-Holland Publishing.
Gold, Bela, ed., 1977, *Research, Technological Change and Economic Analysis,* Lexington, Mass.: Lexington Books.
_____, 1979, *Productivity, Technology and Capital,* Lexington, Mass.: Lexington Books.
Griliches, Zvi, and Dale W. Jorgenson, 1966, "Sources of Measured Productivity Change: Capital Input," *American Economic Review* 56, no. 2:50–61.
Jorgenson, Dale W., and Zvi Griliches, 1967, "The Explanation of Productivity Change," *Review of Economic Studies* 34, no. 99:249–83.
Kendrick, John W., 1956, "Productivity Trends: Capital and Labor," *Review of Economics and Statistics* 38, no. 3:248–57.
Kendrick, John W., and Beatrice N. Vaccara, eds., 1980, *New Developments in Productivity Measurement and Analysis,* National Bureau of Economic Research, Studies in Income and Wealth, vol. 41, Chicago: University of Chicago Press.
Moon, I. Douglas, 1979, "Effect of Sectoral Optimization on Structural Stability of a Single Period Dynamic Input-Output System," *IEEE Transactions on Systems Man and Cybernetics* SMC-9, no. 11:728–32.
Solow, Robert M., 1957, "Technical Change and the Aggregate Production Function," *Review of Economics and Statistics* 39, no. 3:312–20.
Stigler, George J., 1947, *Trends in Output and Employment,* New York: National Bureau of Economic Research.
Tinbergen, Jan, 1942, "Zur Theorie der Langfristigen Wirtsschaftsentwicklung," *Weltwirtsschaftliches Archiv* 55, no. 1:511–49.

I METHODOLOGICAL APPROACHES

2 METHODOLOGICAL ISSUES IN AGGREGATE PRODUCTIVITY ANALYSIS

Ephraim F. Sudit and Nachum Finger

2.1. THE CONCEPT OF TOTAL FACTOR PRODUCTIVITY

Total factor productivity (TFP) has been termed by Abramovitz "a measure of our ignorance" and by Domar the "residual." This terminology alludes to the basic, inevitable fact that productivity is conceptualized and defined to reflect, in aggregate, whatever is not understood or is misunderstood about sources of growth in real output. In other words, given our present state of knowledge and data availability, the sum total of the portion of growth in real output that cannot be accounted for by changes in specific identifiable inputs is thrown into the productivity "wastebasket."

Many of the difficulties of productivity analysis can be traced to this indirect conceptualization and measurement of productivity as our residual ignorance. By definition, we cannot explain what we do not know. Thus, public exhortations for deliberate efforts to "improve" the rate of growth in aggregate productivity suffer from an underlying contradiction in logic. We simply cannot hope to affect consciously something that is defined to measure our lack of knowledge.

Denoting vectors by the ~ sign, consider a production system completely defined by an implicit multi-input multi-output production function F:

$$F(\underset{\sim}{Y}, \underset{\sim}{X}) = 0, \tag{2.1}$$

where $\underset{\sim}{Y} = (Y_1, Y_2, \ldots, Y_m)$, $\underset{\sim}{X} = (X_1, X_2, \ldots, X_n)$. $\underset{\sim}{X}$ and $\underset{\sim}{Y}$ are respectively n-component real input and m-component real output vectors. F represents the technological state of the art. Inputs in production and productivity analysis represent a volume flow of services, for example, man-hours for labor and machine hours for capital (for a more detailed discussion of definitional and measurement problems relating to outputs and capital inputs, see sections 2.7 and 2.8).

In a world of complete certainty and perfect knowledge, it would be possible to identify all tangible and intangible inputs and outputs and to specify their precise interrelationship, F. Consequently, our ignorance residual would be reduced to zero, and any need to refer to the mysteriously vague concept of productivity would be eliminated. Studies by Jorgenson and Griliches (1967, 1972), Christensen and Jorgenson (1970), and Denison (1969), as well as the communications between these researchers, resulted in the introduction of important modifications relating to the appropriate measurement of the capital input and choice of TFP indexes by Jorgenson and Griliches, relative to more conventional approaches pursued by Denison (1962, 1974) and Kendrick (1961, 1973).

2.2. THE SEPARABILITY ASSUMPTION

The basic assumption behind most theoretical and applied productivity analyses is the separability assumption, which stipulates that the production-possibilities set can be represented by a separable transformation surface defined by an equality between aggregate levels of inputs and outputs obtained by their respective separate underlying aggregator functions g and f. Mathematically, this assumption allows the specification of (2.1) as

$$g(\underset{\sim}{Y}) = f(\underset{\sim}{X}). \tag{2.2}$$

The separability assumption is economically restrictive since most production processes, particularly on the aggregate level, probably do not in general exhibit independence of input and output substitution rates along the efficiency frontiers. In a complex technology, changes in the input-possibilities functions are likely to affect output-possibilities functions. Diewert (1976) has proposed an analytical framework dispensing with this assumption at the cost of increased computational complexity. This procedure also calls for a successive singling out of outputs with results marginally dependent on the ordering of the output. Most productivity studies have resorted to diverse versions of the separability assumption since it greatly facilitates specification and estimation of multi-input single-output or multi-unit and multi-output production functions or productivity indexes. Bruno (1978) and Diewert (1978) provide good discussions of the particular assumptions required for reducing a multi-output production function to a single-output net-value-added function. Hasenkamp (1976) offers a good discussion of multi-output multi-input specification and estimation.

2.3. PRODUCTIVITY AND TECHNICAL CHANGE

Productivity change and technical change have become synonymous terms in macroeconomic production analysis. Solow (1957) set the trend by conceptualizing productivity change as a shift of the production function over time, as distinct from movements along the production function attributable to increases in inputs. Most students of productivity adopted his approach (see, e.g., Jorgenson and Griliches, 1967; Christensen and Jorgenson, 1970; Hulten, 1975, 1979).

This conceptualization of productivity advances as technical progress, while firmly linking productivity analysis with an underlying productivity theory, is not free of problems. Operating along a production-possibilities frontier assumes the prevalence of technical efficiency (i.e., efficiency itself becomes part of the revealed technology). The empirical problems associated with this assumption are obvious. What if the production system measured is inefficient and thus "nonrepresentative" of the underlying technology? Suppose factors of production are employed wastefully because of incompetence, x inefficiencies (see Leibenstein, 1966, 1975), bounded rationality (see Simon, 1955), or expense-preference behavior. Changes in the degree of inefficiencies will affect a broadly defined measure of productivity, but will not necessarily affect technical change. These problems are particularly acute on the macro level, where it often stretches credulity to the limit to assume that all or most agents in an economy or in industry either can be or are motivated to produce efficiently. Denison (1962, 1974) makes some allowance for the effect on output of variations in the efficiency of resource allocations in his national growth accountancy framework; however, his analysis in this area is limited to selective inefficiencies.

2.4. TOTAL FACTOR PRODUCTIVITY INDEXES

Numerous "early generation" productivity studies (e.g., Abramovitz, 1956; Fabricant, 1942; Denison, 1962, 1974; Kendrick, 1961, 1973) used modified Laspeyres or Paasche TFP indexes. Factor prices were assigned as weights to the respective inputs to obtain total factor input aggregates. These factor price weights were kept quasi-fixed relative to several selected base years. The input aggregator functions underlying these TFP measures are linearly homogeneous additive production functions. As observed by Nadiri (1970), a constant return-to-scale, constant elasticity of substitution (CES) function is consistent with Kendrick's underlying total factor input function. For an interesting discussion of this point, see also Kendrick and Sato (1963).

Common to most of these productivity studies is the use of a single-output measure (either real GNP or NNP) obtained in the process of national income statistics computations by a simple straightforward addition of output components. The resulting TFP measures of total output-input ratio are thus asymmetric and subject to possible aggregation bias (see section 2.6 for a separate discussion of aggregation biases).

Modified Laspeyres, Paasche, or geometric indexes of the type referred to above suffer from inherent index number biases either overestimating or underestimating changes in TFP aggregates. Also, such input quantity indexes do not conform to Fisher's (1922) reversal rule (i.e., the product of the factor price and the quantity indexes should yield the total cost ratio between any two periods), which is a desirable property for appropriate separation of price and quantity effects. To correct for these index measurement deficiencies, "second generation" productivity studies (e.g., Solow, 1957; Jorgenson and Griliches, 1967; Christensen and Jorgenson, 1970; Hulten, 1975, 1979; Star, 1974) usually use Divisia (1926) input and output indexes. Solow (1957) was among the first to show that Divisia TFP index forms can be naturally derived from simple production relationships.

Divisia indexes have a number of attractive properties. They can be shown to be unbiased subject to certain assumptions regarding underlying production, thereby eliminating index-number biases related to base-year choices. Divisia indexes also exhibit the reproductive property. A discrete Divisia index of discrete Divisia indexes is a discrete Divisia index of the components. The latter property is particularly important for macro-level analysis where aggregate variables are obtained by means of aggregation of subaggregates. Finally, Divisia indexes conform to Fisher's reversal rule.

The derivation of continuous Divisia indexes is relatively simple. Assuming competitive markets for all outputs and all factors of production (including capital), we obtain the following equation of total costs and revenues:

$$\sum_{j=1}^{m} P_j Y_j = \sum_{i=1}^{n} W_i X_i, \tag{2.3}$$

where P_j and W_i are the unit prices of the jth output and the ith input, respectively. The assumptions behind (2.3) are generally less restrictive for the macro level, translating to national product at factor prices being equal to national income.

Totally differentiating (2.3) with respect to time, we obtain

$$\sum_{j=1}^{m} \dot{P}_j Y_j + \sum_{j=1}^{m} P_j \dot{Y}_j = \sum_{i=1}^{n} \dot{W}_i X_i + \sum_{i=1}^{n} W_i \dot{X}_i, \tag{2.4}$$

where " $\cdot$ " denotes differentiation with respect to time. Dividing and multiplying each term in (2.3) by the base-level value of its respective changing variable, and then dividing the right-hand and left-hand sides of equation (2.3) by $\Sigma_{i=1}^{n} W_i X_i$ and $\Sigma_{j=1}^{m} P_j Y_j$, respectively, and rearranging, we get

$$\sum_{j=1}^{m} \frac{\dot{Y}_j}{Y_j} \beta_j - \sum_{i=1}^{n} \frac{\dot{X}_i}{X_i} \alpha_i = \sum_{i=1}^{n} \frac{\dot{W}_i}{W_i} \alpha_i - \sum_{j=1}^{m} \frac{\dot{P}_j}{P_j} \beta_j, \tag{2.5}$$

where

$$\alpha_1 = \frac{W_i X_i}{\Sigma_{i=1}^{n} W_i X_i}$$

is the share of the cost of the ith input in total factor cost and

$$\beta_j = \frac{P_j Y_j}{\Sigma_{j=1}^{n} P_j Y_j}$$

is the share of the revenue of the jth output in total revenues.

The left-hand expression in (2.5)—the difference between the sums of the weighted changes in the quantities of outputs and inputs—is by definition the continuous expression for the percentage change in the TFP Divisia index. The expression in (2.5) reflects the duality between changes in quantities and unit prices. Thus, the percentage changes in TFP could be expressed as the differences in the sums of percentage changes in weighted unit input prices and output prices. Rearrangement of (2.5) reveals that Divisia indexes conform with Fisher's reversal rule.

2.5. UNBIASED AND UNIQUE DISCRETE APPROXIMATIONS TO TFP INDEXES

The expressions for changes in TFP Divisia indexes derived in (2.5) are appropriate for infinitesimal changes. Empirically, time series of cross-sectional economic data are available at discrete intervals. Thus, the choice and use of appropriate general unbiased and unique discrete approximations to continuous form constitute a problem of no small importance in productivity research.

Laspeyres or Paasche indexes are formulated in discrete terms. As pointed out earlier, it can be shown that they are likely to produce biased approximations to their underlying continuous additive aggregator functions. As for the Divisia TFP index, if we denote its path over the time interval (O, T) as $\gamma(t)$, then, following (2.5), we can express its continuous form over (O, T), TFP (O, T) as

$$\text{TFP}\,(O, T) = \exp\{\phi_O^T\left[\sum_j \frac{\dot{Y}_j(t)}{Y_j(t)}\,\beta_j(t) - \sum_i \frac{\dot{X}_i(t)}{X_i(t)}\,\alpha_i(t)\right]d\gamma(t)\}. \qquad (2.6)$$

The Divisia index TFP (O, T) thus represents a set of paths (t) over the time interval (O, T). Being a line integral, it is path-dependent, which gives rise to the problem of cycling (i.e., indicating a range of values for the same input-output technical changes).

To guarantee uniqueness or the absence of cycling, TFP (O, T) has to be path-independent. Hulten (1973) has shown that the necessary and sufficient conditions for path independence are as follows:

1. The existence of total factor input and total factor output aggregates;
2. Linear homogeneity of the aggregates in condition (1) above;
3. The existence of normalized value shares, α_i's and β_j's for aggregate components that are observable and unique up to a scalar multiplication.

Of the above conditions, the first is relatively nonrestrictive since it merely requires that a true value be associated with the index components; the second and third are potentially restrictive. For a single output case, condition 2 reduces to a constant returns-to-scale requirement. Condition 3 requires profit-maximization behavior on the part of production agents; otherwise, the uniqueness of the α_i's and β_j's cannot be guaranteed. This latter condition for optimal behavior may be less restrictive for macroeconomic settings than for individual firms or industries.

Following Tornqvist (1936) and Theil (1968), the discrete counterpart of (2.5) is generally recommended for TFP Divisia indexes as follows:

$$\frac{\text{TFP}_{t+1}}{\text{TFP}_t} = \frac{\sum_{j=1}^{m} \frac{1}{2} (\beta_{jt} + \beta_{j,\,t+1}) \log \left(\frac{Y_{j,t+1}}{Y_{j,\,t}}\right)}{\sum_{i=1}^{n} \frac{1}{2} (\alpha_{it} + \alpha_{i,t+1}) \log \left(\frac{X_{i,t+1}}{X_{i,\,t}}\right)} .$$ (2.7)

Diewert (1976) has shown that the Tornqvist TFP quantity index in (2.7) is exact for a linearly homogeneous translog aggregator function. This is an attractive property since a linearly homogeneous translog function has been shown by Christensen, Jorgenson, and Lau (1973) to be a second-order local approximation to an arbitrary twice-continuous differentiable linear homogeneous function (see section 2.9 for a detailed discussion of the translog function). Consequently, researchers using Divisia TFP indexes cannot be "accused," within the limits of second-order approximation, of arbitrarily prechoosing restrictive underlying production structures. This explains in part the extensive use of Divisia indexes in recent productivity research (see, e.g., Christensen and Jorgenson, 1970; Star, 1974; Hulten, 1979).

2.6. AGGREGATION BIASES

If components of an aggregate that vary proportionately are simply added, the variation in the aggregate will not be biased. In most dynamic production processes, the proportionate assumption rarely holds. Industrial development, for example, is often characterized by increasing capital intensity brought about by almost continuous substitution of labor inputs for capital inputs over time.

Consequently, in macro-productivity analysis, if we use improperly aggregated data (i.e., input or output components that were added together without using explicit weights), as is often the case, then possible biases in input and output portions may result. As shown by Star (1974), the bias can be measured by the correct disaggregate change measure of, say, the inputs $\dot{X}/X$ and the improper aggregate change $\dot{X}^*/X^*$:

$$\frac{\dot{X}^*}{X^*} - \frac{\dot{X}}{X} = \Sigma_i \, \alpha_i \left(\frac{\Sigma_i \, \dot{X}_i}{\Sigma_i \, X_i}\right) - \Sigma_i \frac{\dot{X}_i}{X_i} \, \alpha_i.$$ (2.8)

Since $\Sigma_i \, \alpha_i = 1$, improper aggregation amounts in this case to straight summation of the changes in the component inputs assigning them equal weights. It is therefore easy to see the rationale behind Star's formulation of the following rule of disaggregating one component into two: Suppose there is a bias in input aggregation. Proper disaggregation will decrease (increase) TFP when the input with the highest (lowest) price or share grows the fastest. Thus, macro-level productivity studies, invariably using improperly aggregated inputs and outputs, are likely to produce aggregation-biased TFP estimates. On the input side, if occurrence of technical change manifests itself in increasing prices of certain technically related inputs as well as their relative growth rates simultaneously, productivity analysis based on improper aggregation may overestimate TFP. Indeed, Star (1974) shows this to be precisely the case for residual estimates for the U.S. economy for the 1950–1960 period. Disaggregation of capital into equipment and structures and disaggregation of labor by sex, occupation, age, education, and race reduce the growth of the residual as a percentage of annual growth in value added from 47 percent to 27 percent. Moreover, changing the order of disaggregation of labor affects the magnitude of changes in the residual's role in growth.

2.7. VALUE ADDED VERSUS GROSS OUTPUT

For an economy, real value added is defined as the aggregate volume of all final goods and services net of all intermediate goods. A traditionally defined national net product adjusted for price changes usually serves as a proxy for such real value added. For industries or companies, the price-adjusted value of goods and services purchased from outside the system are subtracted from gross output (total revenues in constant dollars) to obtain real value added. The relationship of real value added to the production function inclusive of all inputs is at best ambiguous. Since real value added (VA) is defined as the difference between separately deflated gross output (Y) and intermediate inputs (M), the use of value added in aggregate productivity studies as a measure of output implicits assumes that the underlying production function is additive-separable of the form $Y = VA + M$. Consequently, while the use of a doubly deflated value-added measure of output in aggregate productivity analysis is convenient from the point of view of macro-data availability, Bruno (1978) and Diewert (1978) showed that it is valid only under very restrictive assumptions with regard to production technology or in cases where prices of outputs and intermediate inputs vary in strict proportion. Apart from their restrictiveness, value-added productivity measures, by excluding intermediate materials from both input and output aggregates, fail to capture their full impact on productivity. For example, value-added–based TFP measures may, to a degree, distort changes in productivity advances related to substitution of labor for energy and energy-intensive capital.

As a result of these difficulties, gross output measures should be used for company and industry studies. On the company level, such data is usually readily available. On the industry level, data facilitating separation between intermediate materials purchased within the industry and intermediate goods purchased from outside the industry have to be secured for gross output productivity analysis. On the economy level, for the purposes of assessing productivity of the national production network, a gross output measure inclusive of all intermediate commodities may be preferable. If the national economic welfare implications of productivity changes are to be analyzed, a resort to valued-added TFP indexes may be necessary in spite of their restrictiveness.

2.8. THE CONCEPT AND MEASUREMENT OF CAPITAL

Few areas in economics are as unsettled and controversial as the question of the appropriate conceptualization, definition, and measurement of capital. Since capital is a major primary input in traditional production theory and productivity analysis, these issues are of major importance to our discussion.

Capital stock is usually conceptualized as a stock of produced (man-made) tools of production (e.g., a stock of x machines). The stock renders a flow of services (inputs) to the production process (e.g., machine hours). In the context of the economic system as a whole, the capital input is an intermediate commodity. This realization raises serious problems with regard to the appropriate interpretation of the relationship between levels of capital inputs and their contributions to outputs. As summarized by Robinson (1969, p. 310), "Looking at the matter in a philosophical light, the reason why there is no meaning to be attached to the marginal product of 'capital' is that, from a long-run point of view, labor and natural resources are the factors of production in the economy as a whole, while capital goods and the time patterns of production are the means by which the factors are deployed."

The fact that capital is an intermediate product raises questions as to whether Solow's (1957) separation between movement along a production function and shifts of the production function (productivity or technical change) is meaningful in a dynamic production environment. Along the lines argued by Rymes (1971) and Malinvaud (1953), capital accumulation (investment) can be viewed as an intermediate good inducing technical change and thereby facilitating consumption growth.

These considerations led Hulten (1979) to propose an effective measure of TFP change inclusive of the productivity-induced accumulation of capital, which he terms the *dynamic residual*. This dynamic residual, in contrast to the conventional residual described above, allows for the effects of capital accumulation by treating investment as an intermediate good and consumption as the only direct delivery of final demand. By contrast, the conventional residual may significantly understate the portion of growth attributable to technical change by failing to account for the reproducibility of capital and its productivity-inducing effect.

It is noteworthy that in a long-term macro context, a conceptualization of capital as an intermediate commodity leads to a significant change in our definition of macroeconomic output. In this context, the volume of consumption goods represents the only direct delivery of final demand to be qualified as output. Investment, a component in the traditional value-added measure of output, should by this logic be excluded on the grounds that it should be treated similarly to other intermediate materials not counted among the final commodities of which GNP components are comprised.

Traditional aggregate productivity analysis inevitably resorts to some notion of an aggregate capital input. However, the very "existence" and meaning of the concept of aggregate capital are debatable, being subject to one of the most acrimonious controversies in the history of the economic profession. In the first place, it seems exceedingly difficult, if not impossible, to define an aggregate capital entity that is independent of the price of capital. The absence of such independence leads to circuitous reasoning that derives marginalist conditions for equilibria interest rates in capital markets as functions of capital inputs and at the same time views prices of capital commodities as determined in part by interest rate–discounting incorporated in their expected present-value estimation. This interdependence between capital prices and traditional quantities measures is also associated with switching phenomena of multiple, input-price–dependent, cost-efficient capital-inputs levels for the same technologies. Pasinetti (1977) offers an excellent review of these issues that questions the existence of the traditional neoclassical aggregate production function as visualized by Solow (1957). Hulten (1979), in his development and estimation of the dynamic residual, addresses these problems only partially. Ultimately, for the purposes of long-term "black box"-type of macro-productivity analysis, it may be advantageous to think of consumption volume as output and labor and natural resources as primary inputs. A more detailed analysis of the process and phases of aggregate production may have to draw upon Sraffa's (1960) analytical framework of "production of commodities by means of commodities."

Apart from the conceptual difficulties, measurement problems of aggregate capital inputs abound. There is currently, however, a degree of consensus among applied researchers that (1) disaggregation to types of plant, equipment, and tools is desirable; (2) imputation of flows of capital services rather than stocks of capital should be used so as to treat all inputs and outputs as flows of goods and services; and (3) capital inputs should be adjusted for degree of utilization and depreciation whenever the data are available. There is less agreement as to how to reprice different vintages, handle intertemporal effects of capital on output, and separate changes in quantities of capital services from changes in quality and embodied technologies for the purposes of construction of aggregate TFP indexes.

It should be emphasized that since estimation of capital services inevitably requires imputation of nonmarket transactions, and in view of the conceptual and measurement difficulties involved, variations and error margins in capital input estimations may be very large. These differences are in turn likely to have a very significant effect on TFP results. The reader could compare differences in TFP results obtained from the same underlying macroeconomic data by Christensen and Jorgenson (1970) and Hulten (1979) and then proceed to study the approaches and the differences between Denison (1962) and Jorgenson and Griliches (1967), who utilize different capital measurement techniques for the same data.

2.9. PRODUCTIVITY INDEXES AND PRODUCTION FUNCTIONS

Conceptually, there is little difference between production function studies and productivity studies. Both implicitly or explicitly specify the structure of the production system to be studied. Solow (1957) has shown that productivity analysis, in a production theory context, could be interpreted as isolation of movements along the production function (expansion of output due to input augmentation) and shifts of the production function (technical change). Viewed from that angle, and assuming a single-output production system, the production function can be written as

$$Y = f(X_1, X_2, \ldots, X_i, \ldots, X_n, t), \tag{2.9}$$

where t is a time variable that represents the shift in the production function over time or technical change. Assuming that technical change is Hicks-neutral (i.e., technological innovations do not affect the technically optimal ratio among the inputs), (2.9) can be rewritten as

$$Y = A(t)f(X_1, X_2, \ldots, X_i, \ldots, X_n), \tag{2.10}$$

where $A(t)$ is the technical change variable. Differentiating Y totally with respect to time, we obtain

$$\dot{Y} = \dot{A}(t) + \sum_{i=1}^{n} \frac{\partial f}{\partial X_i} \dot{X}_i. \tag{2.11}$$

Rearranging (2.11), we get

$$\frac{\dot{A}(t)}{A(t)} = \frac{\dot{Y}}{Y} - \sum_{i=1}^{n} \frac{\partial f}{\partial X_i} \cdot \frac{\dot{X}_i}{Y} \cdot \frac{X_i}{X_i}. \tag{2.12}$$

Assuming profit-maximization behavior, $(\partial f)/(\partial X_i) = W_i/P$, for all i:

$$\frac{\dot{A}(t)}{A(t)} = \frac{\dot{Y}}{Y} - \sum_{i=1}^{n} \frac{W_i X_i}{P\,Y} \frac{\dot{X}_i}{X_i} = \frac{\dot{Y}}{Y} - \sum_{i=1}^{n} \alpha_i \frac{\dot{X}_i}{X_i}. \tag{2.13}$$

The technical change continuous expression for $[\dot{A}(t)]/[A(t)]$ in (2.13) is analogous to the Divisia continuous expression for TFP change in (2.5). Since the sum of the cost shares is unity, $\Sigma_{i=1}^{n}\alpha_i = 1$, the underlying production function is assumed to be linearly homogeneous or exhibiting constant returns to scale.

The production function in (2.10) can therefore be estimated either econometrically or through computation of TFP indexes. The major relative advantage of TFP indexes is that they do not require resort to statistical estimation techniques. For the production function in (2.9) or (2.10) to be estimated econometrically through a variety of least-square methods, it is statistically necessary to assume that all systematic explanatory factors have been properly accounted for. This defies the rationale behind the concept of TFP as a residual measure of our ignorance. Given that our state of knowledge of macro-production systems, in particular, does not permit complete specification of all systematic explanatory variables and full characterization of the nature of technical change, estimates of aggregate production functions are likely to produce estimates of production parameters of very dubious economic meaning.

The suspicion as to the precise economic meaning of statistical estimates of aggregate production function parameters is aggravated by the fact that in most macro-production studies, following the practice established by Cobb and Douglas, time is very often used as a proxy for technical change in macro-productivity studies. It is important to emphasize in this context that conceptual equation of technical change as a shift in the production function over time does not imply the use of time as a proxy for the specification of technical change for the purposes of econometric specification. Time as a technical change variable portrays very smooth and monotonous rates of change in the impact of technical change on output and invariably excludes cycles and reinforcing chain effects in the diffusion of innovations.

On a micro level, adequate specification of technical change inputs in production function research requires detailed engineering knowledge of the technical innovation process. Such knowledge is rarely available on the firm level, let alone on an industry or a macroeconomic basis.

At best, complete engineering characterization of technology inputs may be possible for very specific disaggregate production processes. It is for these micro quasi-engineering production systems that the econometric production function may be a most helpful auxiliary tool.

Apart from the problem of the appropriate proxy for technology, correct econometric specification of the technological structure requires precise distinction between embodied and disembodied technical change, as well as between scale-related and scale-independent technological change. Anything short of relatively precise characterization of technology will impair the economic and statistical validity and reliability of empirical findings.

Numerous attempts have been made at specifications of embodied technology, mainly through input augmentation (see, e.g., Nerlove, 1963; Beckman and Sato, 1969; Fishelson, 1977). Most of these specifications use relatively crude proxies for augmentation, with adverse effects on the quality of the findings. TFP index measurements allow for embodied effects only through changes in input prices that in turn change the weights assigned for aggregation. Increase in input quality would presumably increase its price by increasing the average and marginal product associated with its use. This does not in general adequately account for the effects of embodied technical change. Yet, in the case of index measurement, the adverse effects of imperfect specifications are likely to be smaller than in econometric production function estimation since there is no reliance on statistical estimation techniques.

Technical change related to scale is technical change, the effective implementation of which depends on the scale of operations. Technical change independent of scale is technical change that can be implemented with the same effectiveness at any scale of operations within a relevant range. The distinction between the two is very important in many policy issues (e.g., appropriate yardsticks for the existence of natural monopolies).

Little effort has been made to separate these two types of technical change in the specification of the production structure and econometric estimation. Recently, Denny et al. (1979) and Nadiri and Shankerman (1979) provided a theoretical and empirical framework for identification of the impact of scale on the TFP residual. There is, however, little conceptual difference between this method and the differentiation between returns to scale and neutral technical change in standard production function specifications.

In principle, econometric estimation of production functions can accommodate multi-output multi-input structures by resorting to the use of multivariate statistical estimation techniques, such as factor analysis, principal component analysis, and canonical correlation (see, e.g., Vinod, 1968, 1976).

In practice, the resulting multivariate estimates are often unstable because of the prevalence of strong multicollinearity among the input and output series. This problem can be alleviated by Vinod's (1976) proposal to use canonical ridge ("joint application" of ridge regression and canonical correlation). For TFP indexes, a multi-output specification poses no problem; in fact, proper disaggregation of outputs increases the reliability of TFP measurements.

The major disadvantage of standard TFP index measurements is the necessity to assume a priori the prevalence of competitive conditions in markets for all outputs and factors of production. Otherwise, the cost shares and revenue shares weights based on observable unit prices of inputs and outputs cannot be economically justified, and the discrete approximations become path-dependent (see section 2.5 for a discussion of these aspects). Nonetheless, in estimating productivity advances for telecommunications, ways of accommodating departures from marginal cost pricing in TFP measurements are proposed and discussed by Denny et al. (1979).

On balance, in view of empirical problems, TFP indexes appear to offer less sophisticated but potentially more reliable methods for productivity change than do econometric methods of production function estimation. Neither method, however, is generally superior on methodological and empirical grounds. Ideally, both should be used for cross-check on the consistency and robustness of the findings.

2.10. PRODUCTION FUNCTIONS, COST FUNCTIONS, AND PRODUCTIVITY CHANGE

Productivity changes can be interpreted as shifts in the production function. By the same logic, productivity changes could be viewed as shifts in the cost function. This follows directly from the fundamental duality relationships between cost and production structures. Specifically, if we denote neutral technological change by t, a common single output production function specification would assume the form

$$Y = f(\underset{\sim}{X})e^{\rho t}, \tag{2.14}$$

where ρ represents the rate of the Hicks-neutral technical change, which is commonly interpreted as analogous to the TFP residual change, where $f(\underset{\sim}{X})$ is assumed to be linearly homogeneous. Conceptually, embodied types of technical change can be specified within the production framework by rewriting (2.14) so that the inputs are deaugmented differentially as follows:

$$Y = f(\lambda \underset{\sim}{X})e^{\rho t}, \tag{2.15}$$

where λ vector consists of diverse efficiency factors applied to the respective inputs to account for the differential effects of technical change in terms of the relative productive efficiencies of the inputs. The t parameter in (2.15) is unlikely to correspond to the TFP residual since $f(X)$ would be generally nonhomogeneous.

Next, consider a cost function specification of the following type:

$$C = g(Y, \underset{\sim}{W})e^{\phi t}. \tag{2.16}$$

To the extent that $g(Y, \underset{\sim}{W})$ could be assumed to be linearly homogeneous in Y, the ϕ parameter can be interpreted as the TFP residual. Embodied technical change can be specified in the cost structure framework by differentially augmenting the outputs through multiplication by a vector of respective efficiency indexes (see, e.g., Denny et al., 1979).

As for the choice of explicit functional forms for f and g, among the most widely used formulations in current research are Diewert's (1971) generalized Leontief cost functions and the transcendental logarithmic function of Christensen, Jorgenson, and Lau (1973). Defining an additional variable, X_{n+1}, as $\ln X_{n+1} = t$, single output common translog specifications for production and cost functions, respectively, would take the following forms:

$$\ln Y = \gamma_0 + \sum_{i=1}^{n+1} \gamma_i \ln X_i + \frac{1}{2} \sum_{i=1}^{n+1} \sum_{k=1}^{n+1} \gamma_{ik} \ln X_i \ln X_k; \tag{2.17}$$

$$
\begin{aligned}
\ln C = \sigma_0 &+ \sum_{i=1}^{n} \sigma_i \ln W_i + \sum_{i=1}^{n} \sum_{j=1}^{n} \sigma_{ij} \ln W_i \ln W_j \\
&+ \sum_{i=1}^{n} \sigma_{iY} \, Y \ln W_i \\
&+ \frac{1}{2} \gamma_{YY} (\ln Y)^2 + \sum_{i=1}^{n} \sigma_{i,n+1} \, t \ln W_i + \sigma_{Yt} \, t \ln Y + \sigma_t \, t \\
&+ \frac{1}{2} \sigma_{n+1,n+1} \, (t)^2
\end{aligned} \tag{2.18}
$$

The time variable t can be measured either as the period number or as the natural logarithm of the period number. Also depending on initial assumptions, various constraints may be imposed on parameters γ_i, γ_{ij}, σ_i, and σ_{ij}. (For example, for Hicks-neutral technology, $\sigma_{i,\,n+1} = \sigma_{Yt} = 0$.)

The major advantage of the use of translog forms lies in their generality. Through Taylor series expansions, they can be shown to constitute second-order local approximations to any arbitrary twice-differentiable functions. Consequently, the likelihood of bias in the estimates brought about by the restrictiveness of the functional forms is minimized. A degree of loss in generality of the translog is associated with its multiplicative form, which requires that all inputs be essential to the production process. This assumption may be reasonable for aggregate inputs, but it becomes more tenuous, the more disaggregate the input specification is. Statistically, translog forms present difficulties for direct estimation because of the multiplicity of explanatory variables generated by the cross terms designed to account for input interdependencies. Frequent high levels of multicollinearity introduce fuzziness into the statistical and economic interpretation of the results. As a result, resort to potentially restrictive assumptions (e.g., cost minimization) or more elaborate statistical estimation techniques (e.g., ridge regression) may often be necessary. Being second-order approximations, estimated translog functions do not lend themselves to forecasting inferences beyond the range of observations.

Diewert (1976) has shown that a linearly homogeneous translog production function or unit cost function is the only differentiable linear homogeneous function that is exact for the Tornqvist discrete form of quantity Divisia index. Thus, within a linear homogeneous framework, the underlying aggregator functions for TFP's total factor input and total output aggregates are fairly general.

On theoretical grounds, a direct cost function estimation of productivity changes is preferable to a direct production function estimation. The former allows for an endogenous treatment of input prices in the production decision, while the latter method does not. Nonetheless, direct cost function estimations pose statistical problems because a subset of the explanatory variables (the outputs) is stochastic, and because there are a larger number of independent variables (outputs and input prices). Both production and cost function estimation can accommodate multi-output specifications, but direct cost estimation is advantageous in the sense that, unlike production estimation, it can be achieved by single equation estimation.

Indirect cost function and production function estimates involve explicit reliance on cost production duality (see Shephard, 1970) and estimation of derived factor demand functions (see, e.g., Nelson, 1962; Eldor and Sudit,

1979*b*) and derived cost share functions (see, e.g., Denny et al., 1979; Nadiri and Shankerman, 1979). This resort to simultaneous equation models based on duality facilitates estimation by reducing the multiplicity of explanatory variables at the "expense" of assuming a priori cost-minimizing behavior. This necessity to resort to a potentially restrictive assumption concerning optimal cost behavior without prior empirical evidence is troublesome. Eldor et al. (1979) suggested sequential testing of the effects of assumptions about competitive factor markets and cost minimization on estimates of cost elasticities within a model framework based on cost production duality.

It should be noted, however, that without cost minimization, it is not guaranteed that the estimated cost or production functions will represent the same technological structures. This should be kept in mind when interpreting the shifts in these respective functions as productivity changes and when analyzing the sources of these changes.

2.11. TFP ANALYSIS ON AN AGGREGATE LEVEL: SOME APPLICATIONS

The purpose of this section is to alert the reader to a number of possible important applications of aggregate productivity analysis on national, industry, and corporate levels with potential policy and decision-making implications. Accordingly, interesting uses of aggregate productivity analysis in assessing sources of national economic growth, the distribution of productivity gains, productivity-based budget analysis, and productivity-based pricing for regulatory industries and nationalized industries are surveyed briefly.

2.11.1. TFP as a Source of Aggregate Economic Growth in the United States

By rearranging (2.12), we obtain the framework for "partitioning" the growth in output into the respective shares contributed by TFP and the tangible inputs. There is a broad consensus among economists (e.g., Abramovitz, 1956; Kendrick, 1973; Denison, 1974; Solow, 1957; Star, 1974; Hulten, 1979) that total factor productivity has been playing a substantial role in U.S. national economic growth since the beginning of the rapid industrialization era around the 1970s. The aggregate estimates of the portion of real economic growth of the national economy or the private domestic sector attributable to TFP range from 35 percent to close to 70 percent for long periods. Average annual growth rates for TFP for the first two decades of the postwar period increased relative to prior periods, ranging between 1.5 to 2.5 percent average annual growth. The share of productivity growth in real national or private domestic output per person was even more pronounced. This empirical work has provided some tentative insights into the major potential factors affecting TFP growth.

For example, Denison (1962, 1974) has attempted through a mix of data analysis, statistical analysis, and selective exercise of professional judgment to account for the composition of the residual through more detailed growth accountancy methods. After adjusting changes in certain aspects of labor quality and efficiency in allocation of resources as well as economics of scale, he remains with an "unshrinkable residual" that he chooses to term *advances in knowledge*. Advances in knowledge, according to Kendrick's estimates, account for 64 percent of the residual and 30 percent of the growth in real output for the 1948–1969 period. Economics of scale account for 21 percent of the residual and 10 percent of growth in real output for the same period. The relative importance of advances in knowledge and economics of scale as sources of economic growth is perhaps suggestive of positive association between two factors, mainly—scale-facilitating attainment and application of some of the advances in knowledge.

Generally speaking, few, if any, serious students of growth and productivity deny the very important role of the residual in growth, whether partially "allocated" to other factors or not. Most researchers suggest that the conventional residual may underestimate technical change either by not allowing for the reproducibility of capital in its conventional form or by its exclusion on nonneutral technical change. On the aggregate level, the various estimates of the rate of the residual in growth obtained by diverse methods, measurement techniques, and for different periods are remarkably close, suggesting a fair degree of robustness of the residual TFP estimates.

2.11.2. Distribution of Productivity Gains and Budget Analysis

An interesting application of aggregate productivity analysis on a macro industry and company level is the analysis of the distribution of productivity gains. The left-hand side of the fundamental relationship in equation (2.5) measures, by definition, productivity (TFP) gains. The right-hand side of (2.5) can be viewed as reflecting the distribution of these gains to all potential beneficiaries. The $\dot{W}_i$'s represent the gains in returns to all factors of production (labor, capital, and outside suppliers). Changes in output prices represent changes (positive or negative) in benefits to consumers and customers. The essence of the distribution analysis is to compare the actual changes in (2.5) with various possibilities of changes in input and output prices in the hypothetical eventuality of zero productivity gains. According to (2.5), the absence of any productivity gains would have forced any and all increases in returns to factors of production (input prices) to be "financed" at the expense of the customers (increase in output prices). Consequently, estimation of the differences between the respective changes in input and output prices with and without productivity gains provides a range of estimates of the distribution of those gains among various categories of labor, shareholders, and customers (for a detailed analysis, see Werner, 1977; Eldor and Sudit, 1979a).

The fundamental relationship between changes in prices and quantities over time could be used as the underlying framework for a productivity-based budget analysis. Estimation of implicit productivity changes in budget plans can be effectively used as planning and control tools (1) to detect areas of expense "padding"; (2) to identify inconsistencies among estimates of various departments; and (3) to obtain advance signals of possible deterioration in overall efficiency. Ishikawa and Sudit (1979) proposed the use of implicit TFP indicators as part of a productivity-based budget and zero-based budget analysis.

2.11.3. Productivity-Based Regulatory Adjustments

In public utility regulation, productivity-based automatic rate adjustment formulas have been proposed and occasionally applied in telecommunications, electricity, and natural gas. Kendrick (1975) proposed a TFP-based formula. On the basis of (2.5), Sudit (1979) proposed the following productivity-based automatic rate adjustment formula:

$$\sum_{j=1}^{m} \left(\frac{\dot{P}_j}{P_j}\right)^A \beta_j = \sum_{i=1}^{n} \left(\frac{\dot{W}_i}{W_i}\right)^M \alpha_i - \left(\frac{\dot{TFP}}{TFP}\right)^{min}, \tag{2.19}$$

where $(\dot{W}/W)^M$ are changes in the market prices of the inputs and $(\dot{TFP}/TFP)^{min}$ is the minimum productivity change standard set by the regulatory commission subject to a rate-of-return constraint. The formula in (2.19) provides built-in productivity incentives, as well as built-in incentives to economize on payments to the factors of production. Its use could also reduce the frequency of regulatory proceedings, thereby realizing savings in regulatory transaction costs.

2.11.4.   Productivity-Based Pricing in Nationalized Industries

A productivity-based automatic adjustment formula analogous to (2.19) can be employed for the purposes of periodic pricing in nationalized industries. Crew et al. (1979) have proposed the following adjustment framework:

$$\sum_{j} \frac{\dot{P}_j}{P_j} \beta_j = \sum_{i} \left(\frac{\dot{W}_i}{W_i}\right)^M \alpha_i - \left(\frac{\dot{\text{TFP}}}{\text{TFP}}\right)^T + M, \tag{2.20}$$

where $(\dot{W}_i/W_i)^M$ and $(\dot{\text{TFP}}/\text{TFP})^T$ are increases in market input prices and government set productivity changes, respectively. $M = 1/2[\dot{\text{TFP}}/\text{TFP} - (\dot{\text{TFP}}/\text{TFP})^T]$. Thus, under this arrangement, nationalized companies would keep half of the above-target productivity performance, assuring built-in efficiency incentives. Economy incentives are guaranteed by the adherence of the formula in (2.20) to market input price increases rather than actual increases. Several alternative adjustment mechanisms are explored by Crew et al. (1979).

2.12.   CONCLUDING REMARKS

TFP analysis is aimed at the identification, measurement, and analysis of the unexplained residual, or the magnitude of our ignorance about the production process. This is indeed a useful pursuit if we accept the Socratic view that knowing how much we do not know is the beginning of all knowledge. More often than not, this type of analysis takes us to the limits of available information. At the very least, measurement and analysis of the TFP residual should be helpful in (1) identifying the portions of output growth that cannot be explained by changes in tangible inputs; (2) facilitating the formulation of working hypotheses with regard to major factors affecting the size of TFP and its growth pattern, thereby promoting a better understanding of the production process; (3) assessing the welfare implications of variations of TFP in terms of changes in the "total pie" available for distribution at the economy, industry, and company levels; (4) monitoring potential for changes in relative performance levels of companies and industries (e.g., profitability, growth, competitiveness) and the economy (e.g., inflation, employment, living standards, international trade); and (5) managing government enterprises and regulated industries on the basis of production efficiencies. Generally speaking, the study of the TFP residual on the macro level can be viewed as instrumental and complementary to advances in the analysis of aggregate production systems through explicit and detailed functional specifications.

REFERENCES

Abramovitz, Moses, 1956, "Resource and Output Trends in the U.S. since 1870," *American Economic Review* 46, no. 2:5-23.

Arrow, Kenneth J., H. Chenery, B. Minhas, and R. Solow, 1961, "Capital-Labor Substitution and Economic Efficiency," *Review of Economics and Statistics* 43, no. 3:225-50.

Beckman, M. J., and R. Sato, 1969, "Aggregate Production Functions and Types of Technical Progress," *American Economic Review* 59:88-101.

Bruno, Michael, 1978, "Duality, Intermediate Inputs and Value-Added," in Fuss and McFadden, eds. (1978).

Christensen, Lauritus, and Dale W. Jorgenson, 1970, "U.S. Real Product and Real Factor Input, 1929-67," *Review of Income and Wealth* 16, no. 1:19-50.

Christensen, Lauritus R., Dale W. Jorgenson, and L. J. Lau, 1973, "Transcendental Logarithmic Production Frontiers," *Review of Economics and Statistics* 55, no. 1:28-45.

Crew, Michael A., Paul R. Kleindorfer, and Ephraim F. Sudit, 1979, "Incentives for Efficiency in the Nationalized Industries: Beyond the 1978 White Paper," *Journal of Industrial Affairs* (Fall).

Crew, Michael A., ed., 1979, *Problems in Public Utility Economics and Regulation,* Lexington, Mass.: Lexington Books.

Denison, Edward F., 1962, "The Sources of Economic Growth in the U.S. and the Alternatives before Us," Supplemental Paper No. 13, Washington, D.C.: Committee for Economic Development.

_____, 1969, "Some Major Issues in Productivity Analysis: An Examination of Estimates by Jorgenson and Griliches," *Survey of Current Business* 49, no. 5, Part 2.

_____, 1974, *Accounting for United States Economic Growth, 1929-1969,* Washington, D.C.: Brookings.

Denny, Michael, Melvyn Fuss, and Leonard Waverman, 1979, "The Measurement and Interpretation of Total Factor Productivity in Regulated Industries with an Application to Canadian Telecommunications," paper presented at a conference entitled "Productivity Measurement in Regulated Industries," University of Wisconsin, Madison, May.

Diewert, Erwin W., 1971, "An Application of the Shephard Duality Theorem, a Generalized Leontief Production Function," *Journal of Political Economy* 79, no. 3:481-507.

_____, 1976, "Exact and Superlative Index Numbers," *Journal of Econometrics* 4, no. 2:115-46.

_____, 1978, "Hicks' Aggregation Theorem and the Existence of a Real Value-Added Function," in Fuss and McFadden, eds. (1978).

Divisia, Francois, 1926, *L'indice monetaire et la theorie de la monnaie,* Sirey, Paris: Societe Anonyme du Recueil.

Eldor, Dan, Charles H. Shami, and Ephraim F. Sudit, 1979, "Production-Cost Elasticities in Product and Factor Markets," *Journal of Economics and Business* 31.

Eldor, Dan, and Ephraim F. Sudit, 1979a, "Productivity-Based Financial Net Income Analysis," unpublished paper.

————, 1979b, "Alternative Specifications of Returns to Scale and Joint Estimation of Factor Demand and Production Functions in Telecommunications," unpublished paper.

Fabricant, Solomon, 1942, *Employment in Manufacturing, 1899–1939,* New York: National Bureau for Economic Research.

Fishelson, Gideon, 1977, "Telecommunications: CES Production Function," *Applied Economics* 9, no. 1:9–18.

Fisher, Irving, 1922, *The Making of Index Numbers,* Boston: Houghton Mifflin.

Fuss, Melvyn, and Daniel McFadden, eds., 1978, *Production Economics: A Dual Approach to Theory and Applications,* vol. 2, Amsterdam: North-Holland Publishing.

Hasenkamp, Georg, 1976, *Specification and Estimation of Multiple Output Production Functions,* Berlin: Springer-Verlag.

Hicks, John R., 1946, *Value and Capital,* 2nd ed., Oxford: Clarendon Press.

Hulten, Charles R., 1973, "Divisia Index Numbers," *Econometrica* 41:1017–26.

————, 1975, "Technical Change and the Reproducibility of Capital," *American Economic Review* 65.

————, 1979, "On the Importance of Productivity Change," *American Economic . Review* 61.

Ishikawa, Akira, and Ephraim F. Sudit, 1979, "Sequential Productivity-Based Zero-Based Budgeting," forthcoming in *Management Science.*

Jorgenson, Dale, and Zvi Griliches, 1967, "The Explanation of Productivity Change," *Review of Economic Studies* 34, no. 99:249–83.

————, 1972, "Issues in Growth Accounting: A Reply to Edward F. Denison," *Survey of Current Business* 52, no. 5, Part 2:65–94.

Kendrick, John W., 1961, *Productivity Trends in the U.S.,* New York: National Bureau of Economic Research.

————, 1973, *Postwar Productivity Trends in the U.S. 1948–69,* New York: National Bureau of Economic Research.

————, 1975, "Efficiency Incentives and Cost Factors in Public Utility Automatic Revenue Adjustment Clauses," *Bell Journal of Economics* 6:392–415.

Kendrick, J. W., and R. Sato, 1963, "Factor Prices, Productivity and Economic Growth," *American Economic Review* 53:974–1003.

Leibenstein, Harvey, 1966, "Allocative vs. X-Efficiency," *American Economic Review* 56:392–415.

————, 1975, "Aspects of the X-Efficiency Theory of the Firm," *Bell Journal of Economics* 6:580–606.

Malinvaud, Edmund, 1953, "Capital Accumulation and Efficient Allocation of Resources," *Econometrica* 21, 2:233–68.

Mundlak, Yair, and I. Hoch, 1965, "Consequences of Alternative Specifications in Estimation of Cobb-Douglas Production Functions," *Econometrica* 33, no. 4:814–28.

Nadiri, Ishaq M., 1970, "Some Approaches to the Theory and Measurement of Total Factor Productivity: A Survey," *Journal of Economic Literature* 8:1137-77.

Nadiri, Ishaq M., and Mark A. Shankerman, 1979, "The Structure of Production, Technological Change and the Rate of Growth of Total Factor Productivity in the Bell System," paper presented at a conference entitled "Productivity Measurement in Regulated Industries," University of Wisconsin, Madison, May.

Nelson, Richard R., ed., 1962, *The Rate and Direction of Inventive Activity: Economic and Social Factors,* Princeton, N.J.: Princeton University Press.

Nerlove, Mark, 1963, "Returns to Scale in Electricity Supply," in *Measurement in Economics: Studies in Mathematical Economics and Econometrics in Memory of Yehuda Grunfeld,* edited by C.F. Christ et al., Stanford, Calif.: Stanford University Press.

Pasinetti, Luigi L., 1977, *Lectures on the Theory of Production,* New York: Columbia University Press.

Robinson, Joan, 1969, *The Accumulation of Capital,* 3rd ed., London: Macmillan.

Rymes, Thomas K., 1971, *On Concepts of Capital and Technical Change,* Cambridge: Cambridge University Press.

Shephard, Ronald W., 1970, *Theory on Cost and Production Functions,* Princeton, N.J.: Princeton University Press.

Simon, Herbert, 1955, "A Behavioral Model of Rational Choices, *Quarterly Journal of Economics* 69:99-118.

Solow, Robert M., 1957, "Technical Change and the Aggregate Production Function," *Review of Economics and Statistics* 39:312-20.

Sraffa, Piero, 1960, *Production of Commodities by Means of Commodities,* Cambridge: Cambridge University Press.

Star, Spencer, 1974, "Accounting for the Growth of Output," *American Economic Review* 64, no. 1:123-35.

Sudit, Ephraim F., 1979, "Automatic Rate Adjustment Based on Total Factor Productivity Performance in Public Utility Regulation," in Crew, ed. (1979).

Theil, Henry, 1968, "On the Geometry and the Numerical Approximation of Cost of Living and Real Income Indices," *De Economist* 116.

Tornqvist, L., 1936, "The Bank of Finland's Consumption Price Index," *Bank of Finland Monthly Bulletin* 10.

Vinod, H. D., 1968, "Econometrics of Joint Production," *Econometrica* 36: 322-36.

_____, 1974, "Ridge Estimation of a Translog Production Function," Business and Economics Statistics Section Proceeding, St. Louis, Missouri: American Statistical Association.

_____, 1976, "Canonical Ridge and Econometrics of Joint Production," *Journal of Econometrics* 4.

_____, 1978, "A Survey of Ridge Regression and Related Techniques for Improvement over Ordinary Least Squares," *Review of Economics and Statistics* 60, no. 1.

Werner, M., 1977, "An Integrated Total Factor Productivity—Financial-Based Corporate Planning Model," *Total Factor Productivity,* Symposium I, Teleglobe, Montreal, May.

3 TECHNOLOGICAL CHANGE AND PRODUCTIVITY IN INPUT-OUTPUT ANALYSIS AND THE POTENTIAL OF SECTORAL OPTIMIZATION MODELS

I. Douglas Moon

3.1. INTRODUCTION

The unprecedented slump in the rate of U.S. productivity growth for most of the 1970s, coupled with ever-worsening inflation, has raised fundamental concerns about the nation's economic outlook for the 1980s. The nearly monotonic downtrend growth, revealed in various official statistics, has stimulated many business organizations and government agencies to scrutinize the problem. In academic circles, both theoretical and empirical studies have suggested a variety of approaches to productivity analysis.

In this chapter, we review a number of theoretical input-output (I-O) economic models with the premise that I-O analysis is a useful aid in the study of technological change and ensuing productivity adjustment at an industry level. The study of technology/productivity changes at such a macro level seems to involve many crucial and interdependent elements, one of which is the interactions among individual industries. Any change occurring in one sector's production mode as a result of technological change, for example, would most likely cause similar changes in the other sectors of the economy. I-O analysis is concerned with quantitative study of such interdependence among various industrial sectors, each sector being defined

31

through aggregating similar economic activities. I-O parameters, derived from empirical data, adequately describe complex transactions between industries, which are normally technology-dependent and time-variant.

Assuming that technology is the single most important factor affecting productivity, we describe how each I-O model views and encompasses technology and technological change. Further, we present several I-O models with sectoral optimization recently developed by this author as a potentially useful approach to the study of technology/productivity changes. We motivate sectoral optimization in connection with technological innovations and proceed to explore its effects on the I-O structure of the economy. Compared with conventional I-O models, sectoral optimization models appear to better represent the "best practice" with new technology of each optimized sector, providing a fuller body of information on various productivity components. This would then serve as a more comprehensive basis for the measurement of effective sectoral productivity.

In section 3.2, we provide the basic terminology of I-O economics in conjunction with the earlier I-O models as developed originally by Leontief. In section 3.3, we relate the changes in industrial technology and productivity to the changes in the parameters of the I-O system. In section 3.4, we discuss several linear optimization versions of the original Leontief models. In section 3.5, we consider a number of models in which changes in technology/productivity are explicitly represented. In section 3.6, we present the models for and discuss the consequences of sectoral optimization within the I-O framework. Finally, in section 3.7, we make a few concluding remarks.

As related literature, Erdilek (1977) recently appraised a number of I-O models in connection with the technology/productivity issue. The study was qualitative and comprehensive, covering both macro and micro applications of I-O analysis. In this paper, we exclude micro-level I-O analysis, but include several recent macro models not considered by Erdilek. Further, we make use of algebraic forms of the models in order to have greater insight into interindustrial relationships.

3.2. LEONTIEF INPUT-OUTPUT MODELS

The pioneering work of Leontief (1951, 1966, 1977) resulted in the development of the first quantitative model for empirical interindustry studies, which has been widely applied in many nations over the decades. His first model, known as the static open input-output model, is a linear equilibrium model that involves the disaggregation of an economy into a number of interacting sectors. The model relies heavily on a vast collection of statistical data to describe the interdependence among sectors and on powerful use of matrix algebra. It serves as an analytical tool for analyzing and predicting the behavior of an economy. It is a supply model, with labor the only primary factor, which determines sectoral output levels for a given set of sectoral final demands. In the Leontief conception, production of each sector should be sufficient to meet both intermediate uses within the economy and final demands, considered exogenous, such as household consumption, government use, foreign trade, and so forth. Input requirements in each sector are assumed linearly related to the sectoral gross output level, and the pertinent proportionality defines a set of constants referred to as *input coefficients*, or *technical flow coefficients*. Major assumptions that Leontief made, which many researchers have criticized for stringency and attempted to relax, may be summarized as follows for an m-sector economy:

1. Each kind of m different goods is supplied by a single sector that uses a single production process, ruling out the substitutability among inputs;
2. Each sector produces only one kind of good, disallowing joint production;
3. Each sector consumes intermediate inputs from all sectors, including itself, by constant returns to scale, or, equivalently, sectoral input coefficients are fixed.

The static open model with the above assumptions can be stated as a system of m linear equations, the solvability of which is often characterized in terms of input coefficients. The net output of a sector, gross output less intermediate inputs absorbed by all the sectors of the economy, is to be balanced with respect to external final demand. Assuming that industry i produces commodity i, the corresponding algebraic equations become

$$G_i - \sum_j a_{ij} G_j = C_i, \tag{3.1}$$

for $i = 1, \ldots , m$, where

G_i = the gross output level of sector i;
C_i = the level of final demand for good i;
a_{ij} = input coefficients representing the amount of good i absorbed by sector j to produce one unit of good j.

Input coefficients a_{ij} can be defined in both physical and monetary units. When defined in monetary units, it follows that $0 \leq a_{ij} < 1$, for all i and j. Leontief suggested that these coefficients be determined as the ratio of empirical input quantity to empirical output quantity. The *fixed technology*[1] used in sector j is thus represented by $A_j = (a_{ij})$, for $i = 1, \ldots , m$. The system (3.1) can readily be converted to matrix form, with the definition of $(m \times m)$ input coefficients matrix A for a_{ij} and column vectors G and C for G_i and C_i, respectively; that is,

$$(I - A)G = C, \tag{3.2}$$

where $(I - A)$ is known as the *Leontief matrix*.

The object of the static problem is to find $G \geq 0$ for an estimated $C \geq 0$. If $(I - A)^{-1}$ exists, the solution can be found by $G = (I - A)^{-1}C$. A given final demand vector $C \geq 0$ is said to be *producible* if there exists $G \geq 0$ so that (3.2) is satisfied. The corresponding Leontief matrix is nonnegatively invertible and is said to be *productive*.

In proposing his earlier dynamic I-O model as a system of differential equations, Leontief (1953b) adds the concept of capital stocks required to augment production capabilities of the economy. Leontief again assumes that each sector's capital needs for a given period are proportional to its gross output level of the same period. Proportionality constants, similar to those for flow coefficients, define sectoral *capital coefficients* b_{ij}. The interdependence between the outputs of all sectors of an m-sector economy in two successive periods can be stated in the following difference equation:

$$(I - A)G_t - B(G_{t+1} - G_t) = C_t, \tag{3.3}$$

where B is the $(m \times m)$ matrix of capital coefficients b_{ij}, and the subscripts are for the time periods. The b_{ij} are restricted to be nonnegative and assumed fixed at any point of time.[2] Thus the model assumes that each sector uses a fixed production technology in terms of both technical flow and capital coefficients. Defining $S_t = BG_t$, the problem then becomes that of finding G_t, for all t, for a given set of C_t and the initial capital requirement of the economy, S_0.

There have been a variety of extensions of the static open I-O system. While some researchers have proposed nonlinear models (see, e.g., Sandberg, 1973) or probabilistic models (Goicoechea and Hansen, 1978; Simonovits, 1975), extensions to optimization models of some type and to the models for alternative representation of technology have been prevailing. We shall introduce some of these alternative models in subsequent sections.

3.3. TECHNOLOGICAL CHANGE, PRODUCTIVITY ADJUSTMENT, AND STRUCTURAL CHANGE IN AN INPUT-OUTPUT SYSTEM

One of the most controversial and difficult problems in productivity study arises in the area of productivity measurement (see Eilon and Teague, 1973). It is generally accepted that the productivity, or the efficiency of production, of a productive unit (an industrial sector for our purposes) represents a functional relationship between outputs and inputs. The output of goods or services per man-hour, the widely known definition of productivity, does not appear to serve as a comprehensive measure of sectoral productivity, especially when technological changes are involved. Gold (1973a, 1973b), who has made significant contributions to the subject of productivity study, argues that the output per man-hour measures neither the efficiency of production as a whole nor that of labor's own efforts. He bases this argument upon the fact that productivity is determined by contributions of many kinds of inputs, of which labor is just one; the others include different kinds of materials and supplies, a variety of labor skills, various types of capital facilities and equipment, and a wide array of managerial efforts to systematically organize these inputs to the end of producing outputs.

Accordingly, Gold suggests that efforts of productivity analysis emphasize the following:

1. Changes in the level of each category of input requirements per unit of output;
2. Changes in the proportion in which inputs are combined;
3. Degree of utilization of inputs;
4. Variations in all productivity components as viewed by managers capable of adjusting relationships among them.

Although there is no single, universally acceptable measure of productivity at an industry level, we consider changes in technical relationships among industries as a suitable measure of sectoral productivity change for our purposes. The term *structural change,* as used in the context of I-O structure of the economy, refers to the changes in coefficients a_{ij} or b_{ij} or both. Under his assumptions of single process/single product/single sector, Leontief (1951, 1953a) introduced the general concept of productivity. His two kinds of productivity coefficients, one for industries and the other for commodities, refer to proportional changes in a_{ij} by columns and rows. Leontief also defined labor productivity, based on labor requirements that are determined in constant returns to scale, at both industry and economy levels.

Among the standard sources for structural change of an I-O system are the change in product mix, technological change, changes in relative prices of inputs, and the change in the gross output level in a sector (Carter, 1970a; Forssell, 1972). Although it may not affect technical relationships for an entire industry immediately, any of these factors would most likely give rise to changes in input structure of the industry, as reflected in an I-O table, and hence to changes in sectoral productivity. In this chapter, our interest is particularly in technology-caused changes in the structure of an I-O system (Morishima, 1964; Carter, 1970a).

The level of aggregation in I-O tables can affect the stability of I-O coefficients over time. This is due to two important problems inherent in aggregating production activities of an establishment level to an industry level: product mix, which depends on the relative weight of each product to be "mixed," and process mix, which depends on the degree of substitutability among materials. Both Sevaldson (1970) and Vaccara (1970) correctly point out that a relatively high level of aggregation would show both stability and instability of I-O coefficients over time. They attribute the increased stability to the fact that aggregation can cancel out the impact of substitutions among closely related materials; the increased instability comes from changes in relative weights of individual products to be mixed. Carter (1970a), who has conducted extensive empirical research on the subject of I-O analysis, contends that a column of an I-O table is a "very compressed summary of a much greater body of information" for an industry, in reference to the product/process mix problems.

The role and consequences of technological change are important in determining sectoral productivity. Technological advances can affect many aspects of production at all levels: changes in intermediate input requirements per unit of sectoral production; similar changes in labor or capital requirements or both; changes in output production; and so forth. In some I-O models it is assumed, often for convenience, that technology is fixed over time or that it changes slowly with a long lag. Technology in recent years, however, has been changing at such a rapid rate, as evidenced in many manufacturing industries, that the reality of interindustrial transactions can be better represented in a model with explicit considerations given to possible changes in technology.

Carter makes it clear that the analysis of changing intermediate input requirements contributes significantly to the understanding of technological change. Although she clearly distinguishes between the structural change caused by technological change and that caused by product mix, Carter notes that this distinction becomes less traceable from the point of view of the I-O system as a whole. Similarly, substitution between processes leading to changes in I-O structure would not make a clear-cut distinction from technological change.

3.4. OPTIMIZATION OF INPUT-OUTPUT SYSTEMS

In this section, we describe some of the optimization versions of the earlier Leontief equilibrium models. Each model optimizes the activities of the economy as a whole, rather than optimizing the activities of each sector individually. The primary purpose of an optimization model is the same as that of the corresponding Leontief model, which is to determine a course of the economy for one or more future periods. The difference lies in that an optimization model considers several possible courses for the economy before selecting an "optimal" course. Further, some of the Leontief assumptions can be relaxed by optimization. The conception and derivation of flow/capital coefficients, however, remain the same as those in the Leontief models.

It has been suggested that some of the limiting assumptions of the static Leontief I-O model be relaxed by formulating the interindustry problem as a linear programming (LP) model (see Chenery and Clark, 1959). As compared with the Leontief model, the LP model considers alternative sources of production as separate activities, relaxing the first Leontief assumption. An activity, defined as a general transformation of inputs into outputs, may thus produce several outputs and can treat the Leontief concept of sectoral production as a special case in which a single output is produced. Joint production in interindustry analysis does not create a serious problem since it can be dealt with as an aggregation (or disaggregation) problem in defining sectors. Thus, the Leontief concept of a sector or an industry is equivalent to the set of all LP activities producing a given commodity group. The more significant difference between the Leontief and LP models is that LP uses an explicit objective function to be optimized with respect to inequality production constraints—the former to evaluate the efficiency of alternative processes, and the latter to allow nonexhaustive use of some resources, if necessary. Labor, the only primary factor in the I-O model, appears as important a constraint to be satisfied as any other constraint on intermediate inputs or on final demands.

Dorfman, Samuelson, and Solow (1958) give an LP interpretation of the static Leontief system. Replacing equalities with inequalities and establishing an objective function, they observe that the corresponding LP version would obtain an optimal solution at the same point where the Leontief model would have its unique solution. The implication is that the static I-O model performs an implicit optimization by itself. The authors attribute this phenomenon to the fact that unless a commodity is a free good, there will be no waste or excess tolerated, and that even if each sector of the Leontief system has several alternative processes available, one "preferred" process picked among them will realize the overall efficiency of the I-O system. A rationale justifying the latter is known as the *substitution theorem*. These authors, among others who have advanced this theorem, contend that such nonsubstitution among processes is justified under the premise that joint products are ruled out and labor is the only primary factor indispensable in each sector.

Dorfman et al. (1958) argue that the equalities of the dynamic Leontief system, however, require the economy not to over- or underutilize capital stocks at every moment. Accordingly, they contend that some proper initial setting of capital stocks must "generate the economy's future along the efficient line without any choice."[3] Having observed that there may be many alternative ways of satisfying the future's final demands, depending on the pattern of accumulating capital stocks, these authors proposed an LP model with the objective of maximizing the total value of the sum of capital change and final demand. The constraints result from changing the Leontief equalities to inequalities. Dropping the time reference t for convenience and understanding ΔS as $S_{t+1} - S_t$ and C as C_{t+1}, their one-period problem is that of finding G and combinations of $(\Delta S + C)$ for a given S so as to

$$\text{maximize} \quad K(\Delta S + C)$$
$$\text{subject to} \quad (I - A)G - (\Delta S + C) \geq 0$$
$$B G \leq S$$
$$G \geq 0, \ (\Delta S + C) \geq 0, \tag{3.4}$$

where K is the row vector of coefficients that "play the role of guiding prices, or valuations placed on the new stocks."[4] Observe that there is some complementariness between ΔS and C. For a given $C > 0$, the $(\Delta S + C)$ obtained from (3.4) may not produce $\Delta S \geq 0$, leading to capital decumulation. We will shortly introduce a modified version of model (3.4) for use in one of our sectoral optimization models. Wagner (1957) proposed another LP model, with ΔS divided into production capacity–building and inventory-accumulating capitals. Capital coefficients are then associated with the former only.

3.5. REPRESENTATION OF TECHNOLOGY IN INPUT-OUTPUT SYSTEMS

As noted earlier, the technical coefficients appear as constants in those models introduced in sections 3.2 and 3.4, although they may vary with the times in practical application. In this section, we consider some models that explicitly attach the time concept to those coefficients. More specifically, these models embody technological changes that are assumed to take place over time. We also describe several other models in which technology and technological change are represented in alternative ways.

Gigantes (1970), pointing out the stringency of the Leontief assumption on technology, develops alternative I-O models generalized to some extent. Although they lack optimizing features, his models encompass such technological possibilities as industrial by-products and joint products. His *industry-technology* models assume that the sectoral inputs are proportional to their total outputs and are independent of the composition of these outputs. Technological constraints on the production of industrial by-products and joint products are considered. His *commodity-technology* models assume that there is only one process for producing each commodity, whichever industry produces it; thus, the producing industries would have the same input structure for a given commodity. Then the input structures of industries are linear combinations of the input structures of the commodities they produce. Combining the two models, Gigantes presents the *mixed technology* model in which by-products are treated within a commodity technology framework, with the ne input structure as that from which they are produced.

Carter (1970*b*) introduces embodied technological changes into the I-O system by the use of LP formulation, without employing an explicit dynamic I-O model. Premising that only incremental production may be governed by new technology over a given time interval, she computes I-O coefficients for new technology as a linear combination of the observed coefficients for two "base years," the initial and terminal years of the time interval. She assumes that capital is required to expand or to replace any capacity under either old or new technology. We let

A_n = an I-O matrix of new technology;

A_t = an I-O matrix for average input-output coefficients observed, under old technology, for some base year t;

ΔG_n = a vector of increments to output levels associated with A_n;

ΔG_t = a vector of increments to output levels associated with A_t, to be partitioned into ΔG_t^+ for capacity expansion and ΔG_t^- for capacity scrappage;

ΔC = a vector of increments to final demand.

Given a specified increment to final demand and the total volume of investment available over the time period, Carter defines the LP problem as follows: to find changes in the levels of economy's production activities with new and old techniques so as to minimize total labor costs. Adding to the problem the upper and lower limits on the amount of scrappage of old capacity, Carter presents the following LP model:

$$\text{minimize} \quad L_n \Delta G_n + L_t \Delta G_t^+ - L_t \Delta G_t^-$$
$$\text{subject to} \quad (I - A_n)\Delta G_n + (I - A_t)(\Delta G_t^+ - \Delta C_t^-) \geq \Delta C$$
$$B_n \Delta G_n + B_t \Delta G_t^- \leq k$$
$$\alpha G_t \leq \Delta G_t^- \leq \beta G_t$$
$$\Delta G_n, \Delta G_t^+, \Delta G_t^- \geq 0, \tag{3.5}$$

where L_n and L_t are vectors of labor coefficients with new and old techniques, B_n and B_t are vectors of capital coefficients associated with new and old techniques, k is the specified total amount of new investment available over the period, and G_t is the initial capacity for time t. Both α and β are constants.

Leontief (1970), in his later model of the dynamic I-O system, incorporates technological change into the system by attaching time subscripts to both flow and capital coefficients. Assuming that capital goods produced in a particular year t are put into operation in the immediately succeeding year $(t + 1)$, Leontief suggests the following balance equation for a given national economy:

$$(I - A_t)G_t - B_{t+1}(G_{t+1} - G_t) = C_t. \tag{3.6}$$

A recent United Nations study by Leontief et al. (1977) is a notable application of projecting the I-O coefficients with considerations given to possible technological changes. The global I-O economic model they developed encompasses fifteen regions, classified by the primary criterion of the level of economic development as measured by per capita income levels and the share of manufacturing activity in total gross domestic product. Over forty sectors of economic activity constitute each regional economy. The objective of the model is to predict the behavior of future economies—for the years of 1980, 1990, and 2000—by displaying various possible interrelationships among a number of economic policies, one of which is environmental. To this end, they project the coefficients for those future years based on the 1970 data.

Vogt et al. (1975) proposed a dynamic I-O model that includes both supply and final demand variables. The difference between these two variables is considered as the variable that causes the I-O system to increase or decrease production. Defining $\dot{G}_t$ as the rate of change of gross output levels and Z_t as the supply rate of commodities available for external demand, the proper balance equation corresponding to equation (3.3) becomes

$$(I - A)G_t - B\dot{G}_t = Z_t. \tag{3.7}$$

Defining the error between supply and demand as

$$e_t = C_t - Z_t, \tag{3.8}$$

the rate of change of total production is determined by

$$\dot{G}_t = Fe_t, \tag{3.9}$$

where F is the $(m \times m)$ matrix that represents the dynamic character of the production process. Under equilibrium conditions where supply exactly meets demand, the I-O system (3.7) becomes the static equilibrium I-O system (3.2).

Under the assumptions that productivity of an industry changes slowly and that the rate of production can be increased by controlling the rate at which labor (considered the only constrained primary input) is added to the industry, Vogt et al. also examine the effect of labor on the change of production level. Using the following terminology—

w_i = rate at which labor is added to industry i subject to management decisions and the limits on maximum rate;

γ_i = productivity of industry i (output of goods/day/man-hour), whose rate of change is negligible;

τ_i = length of workday in industry i;

p_i = number of workers in industry i—

the authors express the production rate G, in output of goods/day, as

$$G = \gamma\tau p, \tag{3.10}$$

where $\gamma = \mathrm{diag}\,(\gamma_1, \gamma_2, \ldots, \gamma_m)$, $\tau = \mathrm{diag}\,(\tau_1, \tau_2, \ldots, \tau_m)$, and $p = (p_1, p_2, \ldots, p_m)^T$. Under the assumption that $\dot{\gamma} = \dot{\tau} = 0$ and dropping the time reference, it follows that

$$\dot{G} = \gamma\tau\dot{p} = \gamma\tau w, \tag{3.11}$$

where $w = (w_1, w_2, \ldots, w_m)^T$. From (3.8) and (3.9), this implies that the system matrix F is determined almost entirely by the management decision on the rate of adding labor w. As the authors correctly point out, this kind of analysis applies only to the situation where there is excess labor.

Hill (1977) extends the above model to the case where the rate of productivity change is increased through the introduction of improved technology. Thus, the rate of change of production in his model becomes

$$\dot{G} = \dot{\gamma}\tau p + \gamma\tau\dot{p}, \tag{3.12}$$

where $\dot{\gamma} = \mathrm{diag}\,(g_1, g_2, \ldots, g_m)$, with g_i the rate at which productivity of industry i is increased. The introduction of new technology is assumed to be subject to management decisions. As expected in this case, the system matrix F is now determined by two management decisions: one on the rate of adding labor and the other on the rate of increasing productivity through the introduction of new technology. The model, however, lacks the feature for describing the interactions between productivity and labor requirement; theoretically, an increase in productivity would lead to a decrease in labor requirement.

Moon (1977, 1979a, 1979b) considers certain technological changes that have manifested their great efficiency in relatively short time periods, as experienced by such manufacturing industries as electronics and automobile industries in recent years. The efficiency of such technological advances may be determined by the relative changes in intermediate input requirements, among other criteria, for a given level of output. When considered within the I-O economic framework, such changes would be translated into the changes in flow/capital coefficients. More important, any industry that has available such technological innovations would undoubtedly wish to optimize production activities in pursuit of the most efficient process. This would then be in direct contrast to the efforts of the economy to balance interindustrial transactions. When an industry operates with an optimal process thus determined, an optimal set of transaction coefficients determined accordingly (which may differ from those projected based on an empirical I-O table) would more adequately describe the industry's transactions. Moon investigates the effects on I-O systems of some sectors' switching to their respective optimized processes under new technology. In the context of I-O coefficient matrices, this explores the consequences of substituting *optimized coefficients* for their empirical counterparts.

The value of a sectoral optimization model can best be appreciated by considering the amount of detailed information that can be obtained from the model. This compares with the grossly defined sectoral activity in those optimization models discussed in section 3.4. The model can further serve as a basis for comparing the optimal sectoral performance with its current or future performance based on the current performance. Needless to say, an I-O model with sectoral optimization describes a course for the economy when some sectors operate in an optimal manner. The more important question is that concerning the achievability of the seemingly conflicting objectives of the two problems; we have interindustrial balance for the I-O model and sectoral optimality for a sectoral model. The term *structural stability* properly refers to the state of the coupled system, an I-O system subjected to sectoral optimizations, which is characterized by both problems' obtaining bounded solutions.

Moon studies structural stability of both static and dynamic I-O systems when the aforementioned sectoral optimization is conducted by means of LP. Models (3.2) and (3.4) are used for static and dynamic analyses, respectively. In each analysis, Moon attempts to answer such questions as: (1) How should the level of gross outputs be changed to make final demand producible? (2) Would this adjustment then affect the intended operation of the optimized sector? (3) In the event that more than one sector performs similar optimization, how is the optimality of each optimized sector affected? In the following section, we present both his static (1977, 1979a) and dynamic (1979b) models and state the main results without proofs.

3.6. SECTORAL OPTIMIZATION AND STRUCTURAL CHANGE OF AN INPUT-OUTPUT SYSTEM

Consider a particular sector, say the pth, that benefits from technological innovations over a relatively short time period. The existing technology would require the sector to consume as much as $a_{jp}G_p$ units of intermediate good j to produce G_p units of its own good, where G_p is the output level consistent with the static I-O equilibrium. With the introduction of more efficient technology, sector p would naturally be engaged in "more-for-less" efforts that can be stated as the following LP problem: Find the levels of various production activities $X \geq 0$ so as to

minimize $W X$
subject to $M X = G_p$: output
$$L_j X \leq \alpha_j(a_{jp}G_p), \text{ for } j = 1, \ldots, m: \text{inputs,} \qquad (3.13)$$

where row vectors M and L_j fully describe the new sectoral technology; W stands for the vector of costs, such as labor cost, associated with production activities; and $0 < \alpha_j \leq 1$, for all j, is specified here to establish the maximum target of input consumption under new technology as a fraction of that under existing technology. All the variables and parameters, including a_{jp}, are expressed in monetary units. The obvious expectation, from sector p's point of view, is to determine a production process with new technology that would produce the equilibrium output quantity G_p, but with less amount of intermediate input from some sectors of the economy. In the following paragraphs, we further motivate the sectoral optimization problem (3.13) and explore its relation to the I-O system (3.2).

An industry's reduced consumption of intermediate inputs could be stimulated by, among other things, technological innovations over resource utilization. Once this stimulus is realistically present and quantified as the usual constraint coefficients, the objective to obtain the extreme point of a measure of effectiveness for the industry at issue is also clear. Consequently, a well-defined programming problem like (3.13) is simply there, with no consideration given to possible input price changes. Although the number of input constraints need not be m, thus considering savings in *some* intermediate inputs rather than in all m inputs, LP (3.13) may not produce a feasible program even when $\alpha_j = 1$, for all j, in which case the current levels of input consumption become upper limits. This is partially due to the rigidity of target specifications on inputs; $\alpha_j \leq 1$ for all j, and every constraint is upper bounded. This rules out the probable necessity for "more plastic" when "less steel" is sought. Moon relaxes this rigidity in his later model.

The results of sectoral optimization are transmitted to the I-O system in the form of fixed but optimized input coefficients to replace empirical counterparts that represent old technology. Borrowing from the Leontief approach, Moon computes *optimized coefficients* as the ratio of *optimum input* quantity to *optimum output* quantity, both determined this time from the LP solution rather than from empirical data; that is,

$$a_{jp}^* = \frac{L_j X^*}{M X^*} = \frac{L_j X^*}{G_p},$$ (3.14)

for $j = 1, \ldots, m$, where an asterisk indicates an optimum value. Because of the nature of constraints in (3.13), it follows that $a_{jp}^* \leq \alpha_j a_{jp}$. Even when $\alpha_j = 1$, for all j, for less strict restrictions on intermediate input use, the optimized sectoral technology can be compared to the old counterpart as

$$0 < A_p^* \leq A_p.$$ (3.15)

The replacement of A_p with A_p^* in I-O matrix A may cause a structural change to the entire I-O system. Denoting by A' the new I-O matrix with this replacement, one is concerned not only with the producibility of final demand, but also with immediate consequences on the optimality of the sectoral problem. Moon establishes the following theorem, implying that once an optimum process is chosen with new technology, it remains optimal with respect to the new solution of the perturbed I-O system, a version of the aforementioned substitution theorem in the present context. For the proof of this theorem, Moon obtains preliminary results as Lemmas 3.1 and 3.2.

THEOREM 3.1. *The solution $G' = (G_j')$ to the perturbed I-O system, $(I - A')G = C$, does not affect the status of sectoral operations optimized under new technology.*

LEMMA 3.1. *The final demand is producible in the perturbed I-O system if it was producible in the original I-O system.*

LEMMA 3.2. *$G_p' = (1/y_p)G_p$ and $G_j' = G_j - (y_j/y_p)/G_p$, for $j = 1, \ldots, m$, $j \neq p$, where $y_p \geq 1$ and $y_j \geq 0$, for all $j \neq p$, are the components of $Y = (y_1, \ldots, y_p, \ldots, y_m)^T = (I - A)^{-1}(e_p - A_p^*)$.*

The net effect of optimizing the single sector p within the I-O framework, if $A_p^* \leq A_p$ include strict inequality for at least one component, is a series of output adjustments made in all sectors of the economy. Sector p maintains the optimality of A_p^* as long as it reduces the level of total output and initially optimized activities by a factor of $(1/y_p)$. What then would be the economic implication of y_p? From the definition of Y, one can write $y_p = k_{pp} - \Sigma_{j=1}^m k_{pj} a_{jp}^*$, where k_{ij} are the elements of $(I - A)^{-1}$, for i, $j = 1, \ldots, m$. The term k_{pp} represents the total amount of good p needed directly and indirectly, under existing technology, to support one unit of good p. The term $k_{pj}a_{jp}^*$ then represents the total amount of good p needed directly and indirectly, under existing technology, to support the total amount of input j needed to produce one unit of good p under new technology. The summation then ranges over all such inputs. Relevant economic interpretations can accordingly be made on the magnitude of y_p. Similar observations can be made on other elements of Y, that is, y_j, $j \neq p$.

Moon next investigates the interaction between two optimized sectors with respect to the optimality of production activities. Suppose that another sector of the economy, say sector r, performs similar optimization under a new technology described by $\mathscr{M}$ and $\mathscr{L}_j$ with cost coefficients $\mathscr{W}$. Assuming that sectoral optimizations take place in a sequential manner—sector p followed by sector r—the following problem is proper for sector r: Find $\mathscr{X} \geq 0$ so as to

$$\begin{aligned}
\text{minimize} \quad & \mathscr{W}\mathscr{X} \\
\text{subject to} \quad & \mathscr{M}\mathscr{X} = G_r' \\
& \mathscr{L}_j\mathscr{X} \leq \beta_j(a_{jr}G_r'), \text{ for } j = 1, \ldots, m,
\end{aligned} \tag{3.16}$$

where a_{jr} are the input coefficients for existing technology; G_r' is the rth component of G' as determined by Lemma 3.2; and $0 < \beta_j \leq 1$, for all j, is for the purpose similar to that for α_j in (3.13).

The following theorem establishes the noninterference relationship between the two sectoral problems insofar as the optimality of production is concerned, the proof of which is based on the postoptimality theory of LP:

THEOREM 3.2. *The optimality status of sector r is not affected by the optimization of sector p, and vice versa.*

As a natural extension, Moon considers multisector optimizations and obtains the following result, whose proof is immediate from the sequential application of Theorems 3.1 and 3.2:

COROLLARY. *As multiple sectors of the static I-O system are optimized sequentially, both system equilibrium and sectoral optimality are maintained.*

Alternative sectoral optimization models can be developed by imposing less rigid restrictions on the use of intermediate inputs. Consider relaxing the restriction previously imposed on α_j in (3.13). By specifying some values of α_j so that $\alpha_j > 1$, sector p may consume more input from some sectors than has been required under existing technology. Alternatively, consider establishing the upper limit of the sector's *total* input requirement under new technology as a fraction of that under existing technology. In all practical senses regarding the efficiency of new technology, the new total consumption should be no greater than the old total. Moon chooses to examine the latter case more closely since it is more motivated and tractable mathematically.

Modify the input constraints of LP (3.13) to a single constraint so that the *total* cost of intermediate inputs coming from some or all sectors, with new technology, does not exceed some percentage of the corresponding cost with old technology. Thus, sector p may now use more intermediate inputs from some sectors of the economy; that is, one tolerates the cost for "more aluminum/plastic/nuclear energy/or solar energy" if necessary to achieve "less steel/glass/oil/or coal," as long as the composite cost of these consumptions is less.

If $L_j X$ represents the new input structure of sector p's production, corresponding to the input supplied by sector j, the total cost of all intermediate inputs with new technology can be written as $\Sigma_j(L_j X) = (\Sigma L_j)X$. Replacing the input constraints of LP (3.13) by the single constraint

$$(\Sigma L_j)X \le \gamma(\Sigma a_{jp})G_p, \tag{3.17}$$

where $0 < \gamma \le 1$, the LP of interest is obtained. One can compute optimized coefficients individually by (3.14). Although one knows that $\Sigma a_{jp}^* \le \gamma\Sigma a_{jp}$, one has no knowledge of the magnitude of individual a_{jp}^*; in comparison with empirical coefficients, some may have increased while others have decreased. Lemma 3.1 still holds, but it is not possible to characterize the magnitude of y_p in the same manner as in Lemma 3.2. As a result, the gross output levels of some sectors may be required to increase, while those of other sectors may be required to decrease or to remain unchanged. Theorems 3.1 and 3.2, however, still hold securing sectoral optimalities.

In his dynamic analysis of structural stability, Moon adds the investigation of possible reduction in sectoral capital requirements through the introduction of new technology. Toward the development of the coupled I-O/sector problem, the closed form of model (3.4) with $C = 0$ represents the I-O system, and an extension of LP (3.13) with the addition of capital constraints describes the sectoral problem. The sectoral LP problem differs from LP (3.13) in two respects. First, the constants α_j, for specifying the upper limit on intermediate input consumption as a fraction of the old, are taken to be all 1's. Second, similar constants that could have been defined for capital constraints are considered to be all 1's; thus, the levels of capital consumption under old technology become the upper limits in the capital constraints. The additional set of constraints on the use of capital by sector p can then be written as

$$N_j X \le b_{jp} G_p, \tag{3.18}$$

for $j = 1, \ldots, m$, where N_j describes the requirement of commodity j, as capital, with new technology, and $b_{jp}G_p$ represents the corresponding amount with old technology.

Computations of optimized coefficients, both flow and capital, are again based on the Leontief concept of linear technology and can be obtained from the result of sectoral optimization. The replacement of both kinds of empirical coefficients with optimized counterparts, however, creates far more serious structural perturbations to the I-O system, which is another LP problem, than occur in the static case. The main complexity of analysis stems from the fact that the initial optimum solution of the I-O problem is directly related to some empirical capital coefficients for sector p.

Moon (1976b) systematically establishes a set of conditions under which structural stability of the coupled problem can be realized. Economic interpretations of those conditions are given. Using linear programming theory, he presents rigorous proofs of the results for the dynamic case, similar to Theorems 3.1 and 3.2 and Corollary. Finally, Moon observes that the single-period analysis can be extended to a multiperiod problem by using any of the many decomposition techniques available to LP. Each decomposed problem becomes a single-period problem. In a multiperiod analysis, the time period during which an industry introduces a new technology becomes an important factor, since the production of other sectors might be affected by that technology throughout subsequent periods.

3.7. CONCLUDING REMARKS

In the context of input-output analysis, we have viewed productivity change in a given industry as the composite effect of changes occurring in the industry's I-O parameters—changes in intermediate input or primary factor requirements or both. Among the factors causing structural changes of an input-output system are the change in product mix, changes in factor prices, and the change in production technology. On the premise that a product mix problem is an aggregation-related problem and that substitutions among factors by virtue of price changes do not directly influence the effective productivity of an industry, we considered technological change as the most significant factor influencing industrial productivity. Accordingly, we described the representation of technology and technological change in a number of I-O models. Reflected in I-O tables as a whole, however, there is no clear-cut distinction between these causal factors for structural changes.

Technological change no doubt affects various aspects of sectoral production. It might allow an industry to use less amounts of or to substitute among various input factors or both. It might also affect both quality and quantity of outputs. The degree of utilizing capacities might change with new technology. By often assuming the constancy of I-O coefficients, conventional I-O models fail to adequately describe the effect of technological changes. Some recent models do consider time-variant coefficients, but they fail to distinguish technological change from other factors that cause structural changes, such as the change in product mix and changes in input prices. Further, these models are unable to represent changes in factor and product qualities and changes in capacity utilization, all of which are essential to a comprehensive evaluation of the productivity performance of a given industry.

Sectoral optimization models seem to have much to offer to the endeavor of developing a comprehensive productivity index for an optimizing industry. Apart from being used in the computation of optimized I-O coefficients, the results of sectoral optimization, represented by vector X^*, would constitute a much broader and fuller body of information about sectoral production activities; the size of the optimization problem would determine the extensiveness of information. A typical vector X^* would include such vital information as qualities of physical inputs and of physical outputs, various types of labor, capacity utilization, capital investment, the degree of substitution among inputs, and so forth. Although there is no concrete proposition to make at this point, we believe that the economywide productivity measure could be made more realistic and representative by incorporating this information on sectoral productivity.

NOTES

1. The technical coefficients as they appear in the I-O model are constants for a given year. When used to predict the behavior of future economies, however, an I-O structure would allow the coefficients to vary with the times. This is because the computation of the coefficients is based on historical data of interindustry transactions or their projections into the future.

2. The same arguments as given in note 1 hold for capital coefficients.

3. The Leontief model allows b_{ij} to be nonlinear to avoid capital decumulation.

4. By treating the combination $(\Delta S + C)$ as final demand variable, the maximal-valued $[S_{t+1} + C_{t+1}]$ is sought since S_t is given. Here, S_{t+1} and C_{t+1} are the m-component vectors for capital stock and final demand, respectively. For further motivation of the problem, see pp. 283–90 of Dorfman et al. (1958).

REFERENCES

Barna, T., ed., 1967, *Structural Interdependence and Economic Development,* London: Macmillan.

Carter, A. P., 1970*a*, *Structural Change in the American Economy,* Cambridge, Mass.: Harvard University Press.

_____, 1970*b*, "A Linear Programming System Analyzing Embodied Technological Change," in Carter and Brody, eds. (1970*b*).

Carter, A. P., and A. Brody, eds., 1970*a*, *Applications of Input-Output Analysis,* Amsterdam: North-Holland Publishing.

_____, eds., 1970*b*, *Contributions to Input-Output Analysis.* Amsterdam: North-Holland Publishing.

_____, eds., 1972, *Input-Output Techniques,* Amsterdam: North-Holland Publishing.

Chenery, H. B., and P. G. Clark, 1959, *Interindustry Economics,* New York: John Wiley & Sons.

Dantzig, G. B., 1955, "Optimal Solution of a Dynamic Leontief Model with Substitution," *Econometrica* 23, no. 3:295–302.

Day, R. H., 1970, "Recursive Programming Models of Industrial Development and Technological Change," in Carter and Brody, eds. (1970*b*).

Dorfman, R., P. A. Samuelson, and R. M. Solow, 1958, *Linear Programming and Economic Analysis,* New York: McGraw-Hill.

Eilon, S., and J. Teague, 1973, "On Measures of Productivity," *Omega* 1, no. 5:565–76.

Erdilek, A., 1977, "Productivity, Technological Change, and Input-Output Analysis," in Gold, ed. (1977).

Forssell, O., 1972, "Explaining Changes in Input-Output Coefficients for Finland," in Carter and Brody, eds. (1972).

Gigantes, T., 1970, "The Representation of Technology in Input-Output Systems," in Carter and Brody, eds. (1970*b*).

Goicoechea, A., and D. R. Hansen, 1978, "An Input-Output Model with Stochastic Parameters for Economic Analysis," *AIIE Transactions* 10, no. 3:285–91.

Gold, B., 1973*a*, "Technology, Productivity, and Economic Analysis," *Omega* 1, no. 1:5–24.

_____, 1973*b*, "The Impact of Technological Innovation—Concepts and Measurement," *Omega* 1, no. 2:181–91.

_____, ed., 1977, *Research, Technological Change, and Economic Analysis,* Lexington, Mass.: Lexington Books.

Hill, J. D., 1977, "Extension to Dynamic Leontief Model for a Productive System," *IEEE Transactions on Systems, Man, and Cybernetics* SMC-7, no. 7:544–45.

Koehler, G. J., A. B. Whinston, and G. P. Wright, 1975, "The Solution of Leontief Substitution Systems Using Matrix Iterative Techniques," *Management Science* 21, no. 11:1295–302.

Leontief, W., 1951, *The Structure of the American Economy, 1919-1939*, 2nd ed., New York: Oxford University Press.

———, 1953a, "Structural Change," in Leontief et al. (1953).

———, 1953b, "Dynamic Analysis," in Leontief et al. (1953).

———, 1966, *Input-Output Economics*, New York: Oxford University Press.

———, 1970, "The Dynamic Inverse," in Carter and Brody, eds. (1970b).

———, 1977, *Essays in Economics: Theories, Facts and Policies*, vol. 2, White Plains, N.Y.: M. E. Sharpe.

Leontief, W., et al., 1953, *Studies in the Structure of the American Economy*, New York: Oxford University Press.

Leontief, W., et al., 1977, *The Future of the World Economy*, New York: Oxford University Press.

Luenberger, D. G., and A. Arbel, 1977, "Singular Dynamic Leontief Systems," *Econometrica* 45, no. 4:991-95.

Middelhoek, A. J., 1970, "Tests of the Marginal Stability of Input-Output Coefficients," in Carter and Brody, eds. (1970a).

Moon, I. D., 1977, "Stability of a Static Input-Output System with Optimized Sectoral Operations," *Clemson University Review of Industrial Management and Textile Engineering* (Spring):49-63.

———, 1979a, "Interindustry Analysis for Changing Technologies: An Input-Output Approach," Working Paper No. 79-01, Department of Industrial Engineering and Operations Research, Columbia University.

———, 1979b, "Effect of Sectoral Optimization on Structural Stability of a Single-Period Dynamic Input-Output System," *IEEE Transactions on Systems, Man, and Cybernetics* SMC-9, no. 11:728-32.

Morishima, M., 1964, *Equilibrium, Stability, and Growth: A Multi-Sectoral Analysis*, Oxford: Clarendon Press.

Ozaki, I., 1970, "Economies of Scale and Input-Output Coefficients," in Carter and Brody, eds. (1970a).

Sandberg, I. W., 1973, "A Nonlinear Input-Output Model of a Multisectored Economy," *Econometrica* 41, no. 6:1167-82.

Sevaldson, P., 1967, "Changes in Input-Output Coefficients," in Barna, ed. (1967).

———, 1970, "The Stability of Input-Output Coefficients," in Carter and Brody, eds. (1970a).

Simonovits, A., 1975, "A Note on the Underestimation and Overestimation of the Leontief Inverse," *Econometrica* 43, no. 3:493-98.

Vaccara, B. N., 1970, "Changes over Time in Input-Output Coefficients for the United States," in Carter and Brody, eds. (1970a).

Veinott, A. F., Jr., 1968, "Extreme Points of Leontief Substitution Systems," *Linear Algebra and Its Applications* 1:181-94.

Vogt, W. G., M. H. Mickle, and H. Aldermeshian, 1975, "A Dynamic Leontief Model for a Productive System," *Proceedings of IEEE* 63, no. 3:438-44.

Wagner, H. M., 1957, "A Linear Programming Solution to Dynamic Leontief Type Models," *Management Science* 3, no. 3:234-54.

II LABOR PRODUCTIVITY PATTERNS THROUGH TIME

4 ON THE INTERPRETATION OF INDUSTRY PRODUCTIVITY INDEXES

Lawrence B. Cohen

4.1. INTRODUCTION

Measures of productivity are based on the relation of output to input, most typically output per man-hour or its inverse, man-hours per unit of output. Productivity measures are calculated for all sorts of productive entities: the job or unit operation; the department; the plant or establishment; the company; the industry; and, by an extended interpretation, the entire economy. As a measure, the productivity ratio renders an accounting of input in relation to output and thereby provides a basis for making comparisons of performance over time and among different entities.

The issue raised in this chapter pertains to the interpretation of productivity indexes of whole industries, indexes of the kind published by the U.S. Bureau of Labor Statistics (U.S. Department of Labor, 1978). Using the Bureau of Labor Statistics (BLS) data as the material for empirical analysis, two general points will be advanced: (1) that output in relation to input —the components of the productivity ratio—tends to develop in sequential linear patterns over time; and (2) that changes in the productivity ratio during the period covered by any such linear relationship may be the analytical consequence of the linear function rather than the result of a real change in productivity.

This chapter begins with a brief reference to several theoretical economic points that are germane to the subject. Thereafter, the results of a empirical analysis of the productivity data are presented. It should be understood that while the BLS data are used for the analysis, there is no intention of singling them out for criticism. Finally, a concluding discussion briefly explores the possible significance of the empirical findings.

To introduce the problem, Figure 4.1 presents the index of output per hour of production workers of gray iron foundries (SIC 3321) from 1954 through 1977 (U.S. Department of Labor, 1978, p. 82). (Many other industries could have served just as well for purpose of this illustration.) The index of productivity rose steadily and steeply in this industry from a low of 77.2 in 1954 to a high of 137.9 in 1977, a virtual doubling in a twenty-four-year period. The data and the graph suggest that the rise was exponential. In the entire period, the index actually fell only four times—in 1957, 1967, 1970, and 1971—and these were only minor recessions in an otherwise continuing and upwardly rising sweep of productivity. This is indeed the

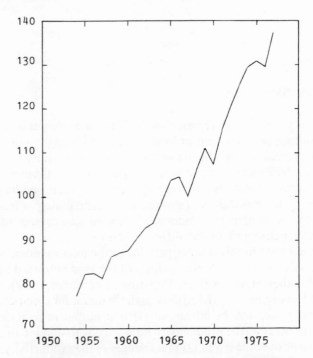

FIGURE 4.1.   Index of Output per Hour of Production Workers of Gray Iron Foundries, 1954–1977

record, and nothing in this chapter will deny the reading of the measure as shown in Figure 4.1. Allowing for variations in detail, similar descriptions can be made of the indexes of other industries. However, if the analysis to follow is valid, it will be possible to see these historical events in an altogether different light, to describe this history in a quite different way, and to perceive the need for a historical inquiry of another kind before the final verdict is rendered on the productivity history of this and other industries.

4.2. THE PRODUCTIVITY INDEX AND PRODUCTION FUNCTIONS

The productivity index is a ratio of two quantities, output and input. In the industry index, input consists of man-hours of production workers. There are enormous data problems to be overcome in constructing such an index, especially, but not exclusively, the homogeneity of product and product mix over time. For present purposes, all such data problems will be disregarded, and the statistics will be accepted and used as published. Nor does the fact that output and input are expressed as indexes, weighted in some appropriate fashion, interfere with the ensuing line of discussion. The important factor concerning the productivity ratio, the statistical problems and their solutions notwithstanding, is the isolation of these two components, output and (production worker) man-hours of input, as the key variables.

The relationship of output and inputs is extensively explored in the economic theory of production functions (see, e.g., Vickrey, 1964). A general expression of such a function may be given as

$$y = f(x_1, x_2, \ldots, x_n), \tag{4.1}$$

in which y represents output and $x_1, \ldots, x_n$ are inputs. For the purpose of differentiating a short-run from a long-run production function, this function is sometimes given in a more detailed form as follows:

$$y = f(x_1, x_2, \ldots, x_n, V_1, V_2, \ldots, V_n). \tag{4.2}$$

In this form, the x's are inputs consumed immediately in the production process, and the V's are long-lasting inputs. Accordingly, equation (4.1) is considered a long-run production function of the firm, while equation (4.2) is considered a short-run function.

A special aspect of the short-run function is also investigated in economics, the so-called one-input model. In this model, all inputs but one are held constant, and the relationship of output to that single input is investigated, yielding the result shown in Figure 4.2. This is the static, short-run model whose contours express the law of variable (or varying) proportions.

Assuming that the one input is labor, the productivity ratio is a property of this model: It is the tangent of the vector angle drawn from the origin to any given point on the output curve. This is usually spoken of as the average output at any particular point. The average increases from the origin to a maximum at the point of inflection of the curve, and thereafter it declines. Average output and the productivity index are the same.

This model contributes two points to the present discussion. It places the productivity ratio within the more general theoretical and analytical context of the production function. Thereby, it also indicates, by reference to the relevant economic literature, that the point of maximum productivity is not necessarily the economic optimum for the individual firm under the particular conditions and assumptions of the model. The economic-theoretic point is that for the firm, the optimal level of output must take into account input and output prices, and that the firm's optimal level of output will generally be different from the point of maximum productivity, usually a higher

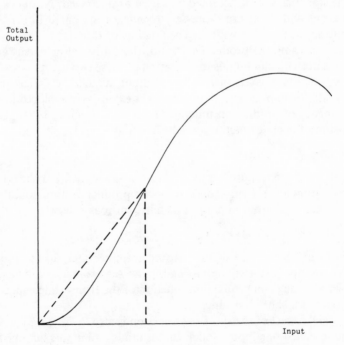

FIGURE 4.2.   Variation of Output with Respect to One Input

point with consequently lower productivity than that available to it under the prevailing production function.

The multiple-input model of the firm's production function adds further results relating to the productivity ratio. The classical two-input model is shown in Figure 4.3. Output can be maintained at any single contour of the model by varying the proportion of the inputs. Thus, at any given level of output, the quantity of labor can be reduced by increasing other inputs. This means that labor productivity can be increased (or reduced) by changing the input proportions within the confines of the short-run static model. As with the single-input model, the productivity ratio remains the analytical consequence of the production function, and the maximum of labor productivity does not necessarily correspond to the optimum economic position for the individual firm.

These models apply to the single firm, but they suffice to supply an analytical framework for the present inquiry. In recent years, considerable attention has been given to the development of a theory of aggregate production functions (see, e.g., Johansen, 1972; Sato, 1975). The data of the productivity indexes correspond more closely to the entity of the aggregate functions than to the single firm. However, there are many complexities in relating the data to the aggregate functions, and the task of exploring them will not be taken up in this paper. This will not immediately affect the ensuing analysis because the framework of the single firm suffices. However, analysis of the relationship of the findings of this study to the theory of aggregate production functions will undoubtedly shed further light on their significance.

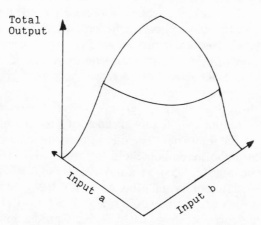

FIGURE 4.3.   Two-Input Production Function

These brief references to economic production functions yield some useful guidelines for the present inquiry. The fundamental relationship of output to inputs is identified and explored in economic literature; the specific subject at hand—output in relation to labor inputs—is shown to be one aspect of the general subject about which the economic discussion has some relevant comment. Next, the productivity ratio itself is the average labor input per unit of output in the economic production functions. Finally, it is useful to keep in mind that the production function theory of economics has a different motivation from the one that yields the productivity ratios. Nevertheless, many of the insights of the economic analysis will illuminate the investigation of the productivity measures.

4.3. THE PRODUCTION FUNCTION AS MODEL

The production function of economic theory provides the analytical model by which the component elements of the productivity index were investigated. In point of fact, no single model was actually adopted as the precise pattern for analysis. Rather, the relationship as such between output and a single input—production worker man-hours—was subjected to inquiry.

The BLS furnishes, along with the productivity index, the indexes of output and of labor inputs—in particular, production worker man-hours employed in its computation (U.S. Department of Labor, 1978). The data include a substantial number of manufacturing and other types of industry, and they cover periods starting as early as 1947 and extending to 1976 or 1977, maximally thirty years. Seven manufacturing industries were selected for examination. The criteria of choice were not rigorous: four-digit industries in order to constrain somewhat the product mix, a mix among the various two-digit groups, and industries of some size. The smallest reported 34,000 production workers. Apart from concentrating on manufacturing industries with these characteristics, there was no known bias in the choice of industries.

Figures 4.4 through 4.10 present graphs showing the relationship of the annual index of output to the annual index of production worker man-hours in each of the industries. These industries are veneer and plywood (SIC 2435,2436), upholstered household furniture (SIC 2512), corrugated and solid fiber boxes (SIC 2653), tires and inner tubes (SIC 3011), gray iron foundries (SIC 3321), motors and generators (SIC 3621), and electric lamps (SIC 3641). On each graph, the year's index of output is plotted (as ordinate) against the corresponding year's index of production worker man-

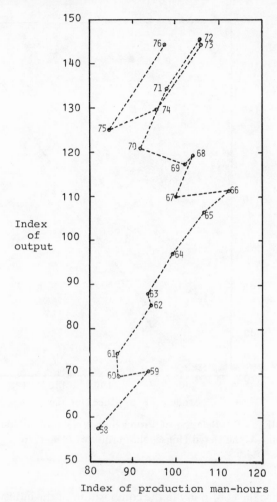

FIGURE 4.4. Relation of Production Worker Man-Hours to Output—Veneer and Plywood, 1958–1976

hours (as abscissa). Adjacent to each point, the year's date is noted. Finally, the points are connected by a broken line in accordance with the sequence of the years. The purpose is to show continuity in the year-to-year data and

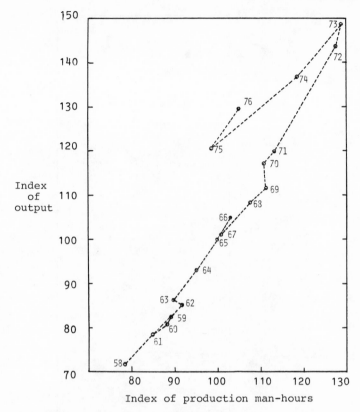

FIGURE 4.5.   Relation of Production Worker Man-Hours to
Output—Upholstered Household Furniture, 1958–1976

thereby to trace the continuity in the composition of the industry. Connect-
ing the years in this way serves also to isolate and to exclude any points aris-
ing from years of different periods and presumably reflecting a different
possible internal composition of the industry.

Figures 4.4 through 4.10 reveal—each in its distinct way—various kinds
of patterns formed by sequential groups of years. The discernment of these
patterns, coupled with notions about technological composition and
change, suggests the possibility of more formal and inbuilt patterns of relationship between output and production worker input. Figures 4.11 through
4.17 present the original points of the preceding figures, but this time

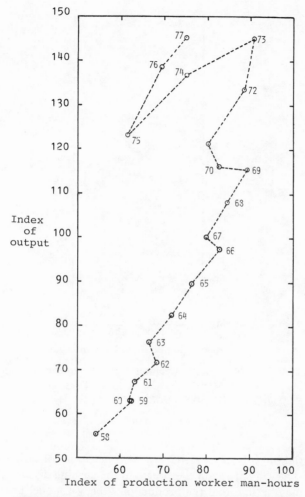

FIGURE 4.6.   Relation of Production Worker Man-
Hours to Output—Corrugated and Solid Fiber Boxes,
1958–1977

formed into series of linear relationships wherever the observed data seem
to justify them. In the absence of historical information about each of the
industries, the formation of these linear relationships remains based upon

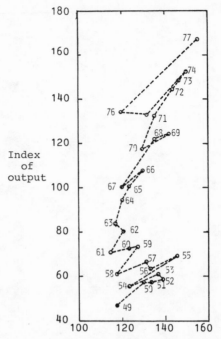

Index of production man-hours

FIGURE 4.7. Relation of Production Worker Man-Hours to Output—Tires and Inner Tubes, 1949-1977

visual criteria, but it is reinforced by other conceptions of technological development that will emerge in the course of the ensuing discussion. For the present, it may be said that the production function model brings to light the possible existence of patterns of relationship between the two variables not perceptible from the indexes themselves.

4.4. THE OBSERVABLE PATTERNS

The revelations of the model may be illustrated by the data of gray iron foundries. Figure 4.1 shows the historical progress of the productivity index of this industry; it was summarized in the earlier discussion. In Figure 4.15,

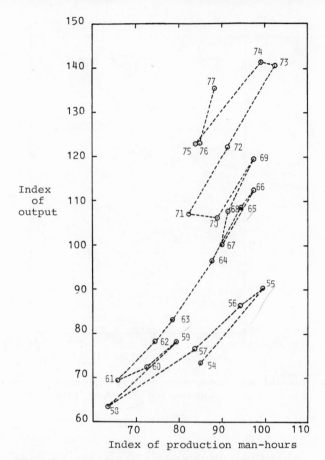

FIGURE 4.8. Relation of Production Worker Man-Hours to Output—Gray Iron Foundries, 1954–1977

the productivity data, disassembled into their two main components and plotted in regression form, disclose a different kind of history. Over the twenty-four-year period from 1954 through 1977, seven linear relationships are identified. Five of them lasted for three years, one for four years, and one for two years. Three points fall outside the indicated lines of relationship: 1954, 1968, and 1977. It is not denied that different judgments might be made about the placement of these relationships, but they would not es-

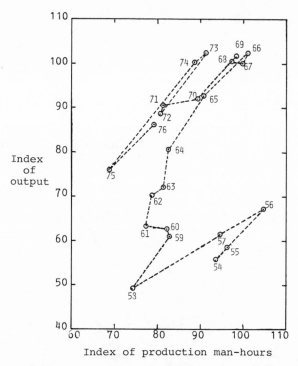

FIGURE 4.9.   Relation of Production Worker Man-
Hours to Output—Motors and Generators, 1954–1976

sentially alter the main points of the present inquiry. Figure 4.15 not only
shows a different development from Figure 4.1; it also indicates that the
evolution of productivity, as measured in Figure 4.1, followed quite a different course.

   This pattern needs the confirmatory evidence of the other industries, as
portrayed in Figures 4.11 through 4.17. Without question, the appearances
of these graphs differ markedly from one another, reflecting differences in
their historical development. However, allowing for these differences in
detail, the evolution of the relationship between output and production
worker man-hours discloses three fundamental elements of similarity. First,
for periods ranging from as few as two to as many as seven years, there are
linear relationships between output and input. Not only do these relation-

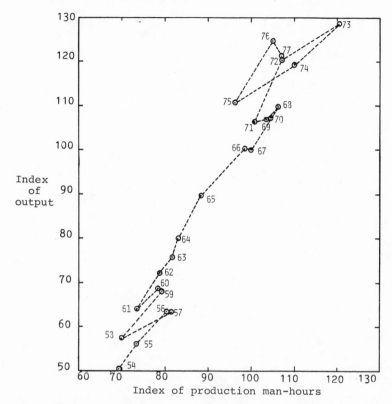

FIGURE 4.10. Relation of Production Worker Man-Hours to Output—Electric Lamps, 1954-1977

ships exist, but also many of them persist as production increases, decreases, or both increases and decreases within the same period. There are some few instances where a nonlinear relationship might be considered, but it is ruled out on the grounds of simplicity, because the shifting back and forth where it occurs adheres to the linear pattern, and because the linear relationships exhibit a marked similarity in slope, suggesting something of substantive consequence within the industry. In this connection, it should be noted that this judgment of linearity covers only the range of actual observation. Extrapolation of the lines to the x or y axis is only of analytic significance. When the intercept is positive, it cannot possibly mean that

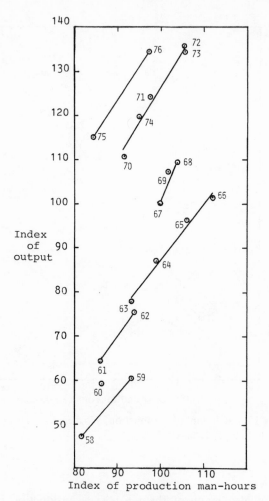

FIGURE 4.11.   Lines of Relationship: Indexes
of Output and Production Worker Man-Hours
—Veneer and Plywood, 1958–1976

production might occur with no labor input. Thus, the linear relationship is
not intended to have substantive significance to the 0 point of either dimension: It applies to the observable range of the points.

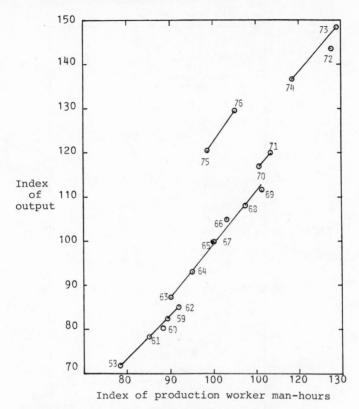

FIGURE 4.12. Lines of Relationship: Indexes of Output and Production Worker Man-Hours—Upholstered Household Furniture, 1958–1976

The second common element among these graphs is the presence of multiple, successive linear relationships, each later one higher than its predecessor. Here again, the several industries used as examples show differences in detail, but the general pattern prevails. Thus, if the individual linear relationship expresses a period of stability in the output-input relationship, the succession of these lines indicates that the history of the relationship is made of successive periods of stability, each separated from the preceding one by some kind of systematic internal change. The history proceeds in jumps that exhibit marked regularity.

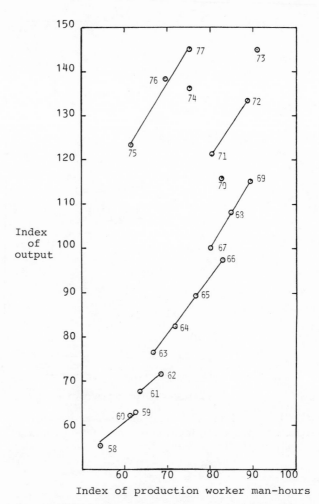

FIGURE 4.13.   Lines of Relationship: Indexes of Output and
Production Worker Man-Hours —Corrugated and Solid Fiber
Boxes, 1958–1977

The third common element among the graphs is the occurrence of isolated points falling between the lines of relationship, but representing years
later than the lower line and earlier than the higher line. They are external to

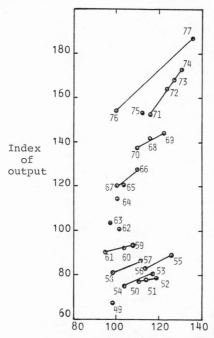

FIGURE 4.14. Lines of Relationship: Indexes of Output and Production Worker Man-Hours —Tires and Inner Tubes, 1948–1977

the lines of relationship both in position and in time. They are therefore not treated as random deviations from an established stable relationship. These isolated points—sometimes a single year, sometimes more than one—are considered as transition points reflecting an intermediate and temporary position of the input-output relationship from one level of stability to the next.

4.5. THE PATTERNS AND PRODUCTIVITY

The existence of a linear relationship between man-hour input and output for periods of years imposes a formal limiting framework on the measure of

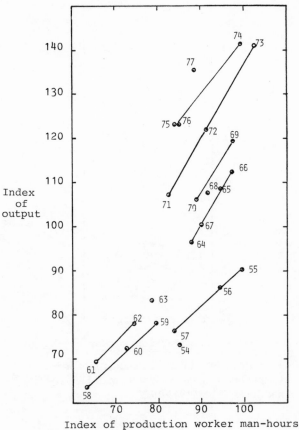

FIGURE 4.15.   Lines of Relationship: Indexes of Output
and Production Worker Man-Hours—Gray Iron Foundries, 1954–1977

productivity during such periods. Where the output-input relationship is
linear, as in the present cases, the average productivity y/x (the productivity
ratio) follows a fixed rule. Denoting by a the absolute value of the intercept,

$$\frac{y}{x} = \frac{a}{x} + b \quad \text{or} \quad \frac{y}{x} = -\frac{a}{x} + b. \tag{4.3}$$

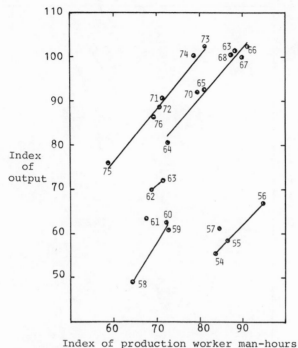

FIGURE 4.16. Lines of Relationship: Indexes of Output and Production Worker Man-Hours—Motors and Generators, 1954–1976

These productivity functions establish that during the period of any given linear function, productivity will amount to a value of b plus a/x or $-a/x$ if the intercept is negative.

This fixed connection between the productivity ratio and the linear relationship is illustrated in Figure 4.18. Here the seven linear functions of the gray iron foundries are converted into their corresponding productivity functions and plotted. The actual productivity ratios of the same years as the functions are also plotted. Figure 4.18 shows that the productivity indexes follow the patterns imposed by their function. They vary with the functions, and functions differ in shape and even in direction.

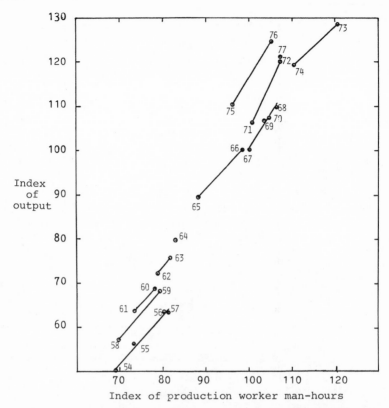

FIGURE 4.17.   Lines of Relationship: Indexes of Output and Production
Worker Man-Hours—Electric Lamps, 1954–1976

It will be observed that six of the productivity functions increase
(although at a diminishing rate), while the top one diminishes (also at a
diminishing rate). The increasing or decreasing productivity function
derives from a single property of the original linear relationship, the sign of
the y-intercept.

Figure 4.18 shows industry productivity in a different light from the one
cast by the historical series of the index and as presented in Figure 4.1.
Figure 4.18 reveals two kinds of changes in the index. One consists of year-

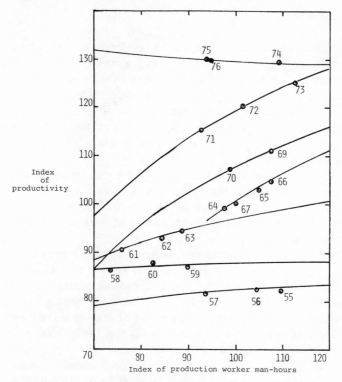

FIGURE 4.18.   The Index Productivity in Relation to the Index
of Production Worker Man-Hours—Gray Iron Foundries

to-year changes, sometimes small and sometimes quite substantial, occurring within the range of a given productivity function. These changes are
sometimes increases and sometimes decreases, but they are still very closely
associated with the functions to which they apply. The other kind of change
in the index occurs when a new function arises. The successive functions disclose uniformly higher levels of the index within the range of actual data
(although the functions themselves often extend below preceding functions)
and observable differences in slope.

4.6. DISCUSSION

The findings of this inquiry consist of the evidence that sequences of linear relationships exist between production worker man-hours and output in the annual data of industries. The coefficients of the linear functions are not important here; if they were, more refined statistical analysis would be necessary. The sign of the y-intercept has relevance to the interpretation of the productivity measure, but this, too, is not a critical fact in the overall findings. The result to which attention is drawn is the occurrence of the linear patterns as such.

The occurrence of these patterns raises the general question of how they are generated and what the regularities reveal about the structure and workings of the industries from which they originate. The best that can now be offered in response will be some suggestions and reservations about the possible meaning of the empirical findings.

There is a simple explanation of the patterns that suggests itself on the basis of the definitions of the data and their known interrelationships. According to this explanation, the linear relations are production functions that last for periods of years and are then replaced by new ones. A single linear relation persists as long as the number of man-hours required by output conforms to the function, which is to say that the technological composition of the industry remains stable. The transition points and the successive linear relationships mark changes in the technological composition of the industry and hence new and more productive functional relationships. The linear relationships are thus indicators of technological stability within an industry, while the emergence of a new linear function signals a change and improvement in the technology.

It may indeed turn out that this is the framework for an explanation of the patterns. But there are some important realistic and theoretical reservations to be overcome before a final explanation is fashioned.

One dramatic problem lies on the surface of this explanation of the patterns. The shift from one linear function to the next occurs sometimes in a single year and sometimes via intermediate transition points lasting usually not more than one year. This would imply that some technological improvement is introduced into an industry and spreads within a short time—a year or less—over all or most of the production units. A priori it would seem that the diffusion of technological improvement would take more time and would show up perhaps differently from the evidence of the linear patterns. There is here a researchable problem: the timing of technological innovation and the emergence of its effects in respect to production worker man-hours.

There are also problems suggested by the theory of aggregate production functions (Johansen, 1972; Sato, 1975). The possibility of generating aggregate production functions from empirical data implies some fairly rigorous conditions as to technology, participation of firms and their relative size, and other factors that are not satisfied by the actual conditions of the data. Further, as Johansen (1972, p. 27) states, "The changes in the short run function through time will be generated by many more factors than technological progress." The aggregate theory also suggests that the individual linear functions encountered in this inquiry may actually reflect a sequence of aggregate production functions, not a single one extended over a period of years.

These considerations and others warn against hasty interpretation of the linear functions as technological in origin, although they may well have important technological components. As noted earlier, these consequences of the findings are proper subjects for further analysis.

The best that can be suggested at this stage is that the empirical regularities are generated out of the economic processes of the industry and that they appear to be expressions of aggregate economic/production functions. Beyond this, just what the connections are remains to be explored.

4.7. CONCLUSION

The foregoing discussion contributes some points that help to illuminate the empirical findings and that leave some matters still unexplained.

First, there is no need to retreat from the empirical results as such. The relationship of output to input of production worker man-hours displays certain kinds of linear (and possibly nonlinear) relationships between the two variables, transition points, and successive linear relationships.

Second, from this it must follow that the productivity ratio should be interpreted by direct reference to its position in the pattern of relationship between the two component variables. In a linear function with positive intercept, the ratio of y/x will decline as x increases and will increase as x declines, a direct consequence of the analytical properties of the function itself. Changes in the productivity ratio should be interpreted in the light of this fact. Further, a shift to a transition point or a new relationship signals a genuine change in the component elements of productivity.

Third, the theoretical model of aggregate economic production functions offers the possibility of an explanation of the empirical findings.

REFERENCES

Johansen, Leif, 1972, *Production Functions,* Amsterdam: North-Holland Publishing.
Sato, K., 1975, *Production Function and Aggregation,* Amsterdam: North-Holland Publishing.
U.S. Department of Labor, Bureau of Labor Statistics, 1978, *Productivity Indexes for Selected Industries,* Washington, D.C.: U.S. Government Printing Office.
Vickrey, William S., 1964, *Microstatics,* New York: Harcourt, Brace, and World.

5 THE ASYMMETRIC BEHAVIOR OF LABOR PRODUCTIVITY DURING THE BUSINESS CYCLE

Salih N. Neftci

5.1. INTRODUCTION

This chapter analyzes what Gordon (1979) calls the "end-of-expansion" phenomenon in short-term productivity behavior. In simplest terms, we investigate whether the decision rules used by individual firms to determine the optimal employment level depend on the stage of the business cycle. To see why this may be so, note that the expectation that a recession is imminent need not be a sufficient reason for firms to initiate any layoffs if this expectation may turn out to be wrong—which it may—and if the costs of hiring back the laid-off work force is nonzero—which it is. Under these conditions, a firm facing a drop in its demand may decide to lower the production without laying off the work force until it becomes more certain that the downturn has definitely started. This means that average labor productivity may show a drop *before* the peak is reached; similarly, once the firms become certain of the state of the economy, they will take decisive action by laying off the work force that has remained idle, and this would tend to raise average labor productivity.

Several economists, beginning with Oi (1962), have previously noted the possibility that labor may behave as a "quasi-fixed" input and that this will have implications on the cyclical behavior of labor productivity (see also Solow, 1973; Sargent, 1978; Sims, 1974). Yet, as far as we know, no empirical study testing for such asymmetry in the productivity series has been performed. But the direction of asymmetry *is* important for modeling and predicting the behavior of labor productivity. In the case of prediction, a model incorporating asymmetric behavior is likely to be more precise, especially if the economy has experienced a deep recession, such as the one in 1974. If there is a bias due to ignoring the asymmetric behavior during the cycle, a sharp recession is likely to amplify this bias and to affect the predicted values significantly. This may be the case of the recent productivity behavior in the United States.

Determining any asymmetry in the productivity series is important from the point of view of macro theory as well, since if labor productivity behaves asymmetrically, then economic optimization problems of producers need to be reformulated so as to incorporate the main characteristic that generates such asymmetries—namely, the degree of uncertainty about the stage of the business cycle.

We study this issue using quarterly series on labor productivity for the U.S. economy and time series tools. The chapter is organized as follows: First, we deal with the expected behavior of labor productivity in the short run when most other factors are constant. Next, a nonparametric test is applied to the labor productivity data to see if an asymmetry exists. Since the test has low power because of small size, we next apply a Kalman Filter procedure to see if the autoregressive representation of the productivity series varies in a systematic fashion over time. Finally, we provide some out-of-sample predictions based upon two different models—one assuming symmetry, the other incorporating some asymmetry.

As a side benefit, the study may also shed some light on whether the recent slowdown in labor productivity is a familiar "end-of-expansion" phenomenon or something unexperienced previously (see Norsworthy et al., 1979; Nordhaus, 1972).

5.2. THE BACKGROUND

Before attempting any empirical analysis, it may be worthwhile to discuss briefly the reasons behind this hypothesized asymmetric behavior of average labor productivity. Besides clarifying some of the issues, this discussion may also illustrate how the asymmetry is related to the "puzzle" of short-term increasing returns to labor. Several authors have previously investigated in detail the behavior of (average) labor productivity during the business cycle (see, e.g., Kuh, 1965; Sims, 1974; You, 1979). The procyclical behavior of labor productivity emerges as the most striking element of this analysis. In an environment where production functions exhibit diminishing returns with respect to labor, one would expect average labor productivity to decrease with increases in employment. Thus, the procyclical behavior of labor productivity seems paradoxical. However, in a richer model that includes adjustment costs, economic agents would be forced to react not only to the prices observed presently, but also to the forecasts of future prices. This introduces lags in the inputs demand functions and under appropriate circumstances yields a positive correlation between employment and productivity even when there are diminishing returns to labor (see, e.g., Sims, 1974).

Thus, the costs involved in adjusting labor inputs emerge as one possible explanation for the procyclical behavior of labor productivity. But this suggests a further complication. If adjustments of labor inputs are costly, then these costs will in all likelihood be different during upturns and downturns. Such differentials may occur in the costs of hiring and laying off the workers. For example, a producer may not be able to lower employment as fast as he can lower production.[1] For a certain period after the output starts declining, the firm may have to keep some *overhead* labor. Under these conditions, a sudden drop in output after the business cycle peak will *not* be accompanied by a similar drop in employment, and as a result, average labor productivity will show a sharp decline. On the other hand, once the firms adjust their employment to "desired" levels, any increase in production will be accompanied by an increase in employment, and there will not be any *sharp* increase in (average) labor productivity. Several authors have suggested that such a process can occur in a world where the production function exhibits diminishing returns to labor and that this would explain the "paradox" of procyclical labor productivity. However, if this is the case, then the econometrics dealing with the issue should separate the "ups" from the "downs." Or, to be a little more precise, the distributed lags in the econometric models of labor productivity should allow this different behavior before and after the downturn.

To make these statements a little more precise, consider Figure 5.1, which represents the isoquants faced by the producer who is confronted with the relative price w/r, where w is the nominal wage and r is the cost of capital. Assume for simplicity that at the business cycle peak, the producer was using K^* and L^*, which, according to the tangency, give the "optimal" input combination. Under the assumptions of neoclassical production theory, (especially homogeneity of degree one), line OA will represent the optimal capital/labor ratio at the given w/r. Since for different levels of Y_i

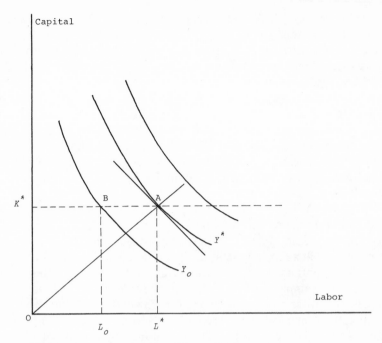

FIGURE 5.1. Isoquants Faced by a Producer

this ratio is constant, the average labor productivity would also be constant if there were no adjustment costs to K or L and if the w/r ratio remains the same.

However, there is general agreement that in the "short run" capital stock should be considered as constant at, say, K^*. Under these conditions, a sudden drop in production will lower the output to, say, Y_0. Yet, if there are costs in adjusting the labor force too rapidly, the lowering of employment from L^* to L_0 may proceed at a slower rate. Thus, the average labor productivity that was originally Y^*/L^* would suddenly go *down* to Y_0/L^*. However, as labor is adjusted gradually towards L_0, there will be a gradual rise in the labor productivity.

On the other hand, if starting from the K^*-L_0 combination the producer desires to increase production, then the optimal route to follow would be to proceed along the line BA. Under these conditions, the K/L ratio would slowly decrease, and consequently there would be a slow drop in the labor productivity.

To summarize the behavior of average labor productivity suggested by this scenario, we note that once the downturn begins there will be a sudden drop in productivity (due to overhead labor), and then as employment is adjusted to a new level, productivity will rise during the upturn. Finally, as the economy nears a new downturn, productivity will show another gradual decline.

Thus, the scenario is consistent with the observed "paradox" of decreasing labor productivity during contractions of employment. Nevertheless, the production function still exhibits decreasing returns to the labor input. The scenario also suggests asymmetric behavior for labor productivity in the sense that during expansions, no sudden jumps in labor productivity will occur. In the next section, we study the time-series evidence on the behavior of labor productivity to see whether such asymmetry exists.

5.3. THE DATA

Figure 5.2 displays the behavior of average labor productivity for the United States. We let $\hat{X}(t)$ denote this time series and assume that $X(t)$, which is obtained by

$$\hat{X}(t) = \alpha + \beta t + X(t), \tag{5.1}$$

represents the cyclical component of (average) labor productivity. Figure 5.3 displays this component. The *downturns* are periods according to reference dates given by the National Bureau of Economic Research (NBER); that is, they approximately represent periods during which employment declined. Thus, in a world without adjustment costs, one would expect the Y/L ratio to *increase* during these periods if there were diminishing returns to the labor input. As one observes from Figure 5.3, at, or a little before, the peak average, labor productivity shows a sudden decline in each case. On the other hand, once this sudden drop ends, the movement is usually replaced by a gradual increase in productivity.

Thus, according to this casual examination, the behavior of labor productivity is not inconsistent with the scenario described above: The drops in Y/L are much sharper when compared with the rises. This is in turn consistent with the hypothesis that a producer observing (or rather forecasting) a downturn first lowers production suddenly and then adjusts the employment gradually.

The next question is whether one can go beyond a casual analysis and test the hypothesis that the stochastic process $[X(t)]$ representing average labor productivity behaves asymmetrically before and after the downturn. Such a test is described below. However, the reader should be cautioned that because of the small sample size, the outcome of the test may be strongly influenced by sampling variability.

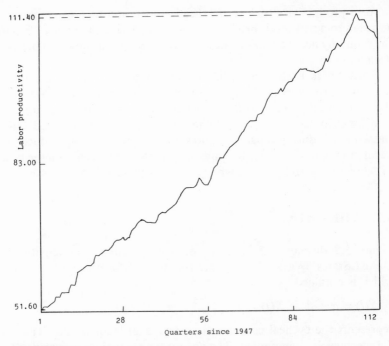

FIGURE 5.2.   Average Labor Productivity, 1947–1974

First, we briefly describe the test. According to the suggestive discussion above, the (hypothesized) asymmetry in labor productivity manifests itself as sharp declines but gradual increases. The process would be asymmetric if, in particular, the process $[X(t)]$ exhibited a larger number of consecutive declines when compared with consecutive rises (see Figure 5.3).[2] Thus, letting $[\Delta X(t)]$ denote the process obtained from $X(t)$ by the first difference operator Δ, we define a new stochastic process $[I(t)]$ by

$$I(t) = \begin{bmatrix} +1 \text{ if } X(t) > 0 \\ -1 \text{ if } X(t) < 0. \end{bmatrix} \qquad (5.2)$$

Under these conditions, every realization of the $X(t)$ process will define a realization for the $I(t)$ process. The hypothesis of asymmetry in question can then be formulated in terms of the process $I(t)$. In fact, a series of consecutive drops in $X(t)$ implies that $I(t)$ will be negative for a certain period of time, while increases in $X(t)$ will make it positive. We denote by *runs* the sequences of consecutive +1's or −1's. Under these conditions, every realization of $I(t)$ would yield a series of runs with different lengths. The hypoth-

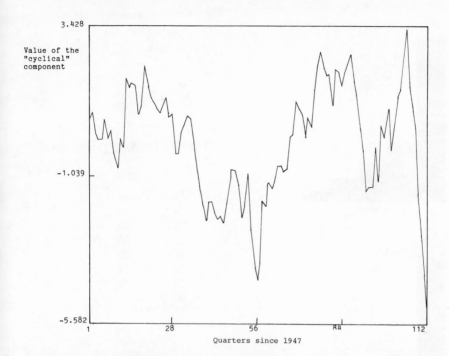

FIGURE 5.3. "Cyclical" Component of Labor Productivity, 1947–1974

NOTE: This figure represents the deviations of labor productivity around a constant and a linear trend.

esis of asymmetry can then be reworded by saying that the $I(t)$ series exhibits a larger number of "long" runs in −1's when compared with runs of +1's.

Figure 5.4 illustrates the sample distributions of runs in +1 and −1's. We observe the following phenomenon in this figure: In spite of the limited number of observations that we have, the tail of the distribution of runs in −1's is longer than the tail of distribution of runs in +1's. This implies that, for the particular series under consideration, a larger number of consecutive declines were observed. In contrast, not as many long stretches of rises were present in the $X(t)$ series.

To put these observations into a more objective setting, we decided to test the equality of the distributions of runs in +1's and −1's. For example, letting $F_{+1}(x)$ and $F_{-1}(x)$ denote the distribution functions of runs in +1's and −1's, respectively, the hypothesis

$$H_0: F_{-1}(x) = F_{+1}(x) \qquad (5.3)$$

(a) Distribution of runs in + 1's

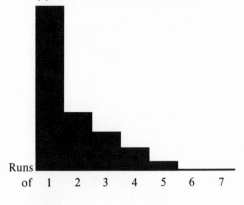

Runs
of   1   2   3   4   5   6   7

(b) Distribution of runs in − 1's

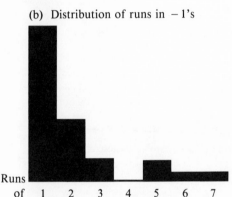

Runs
of   1   2   3   4   5   6   7

(c) The values of $S_{-1}(x)$ and $S_{+1}(x)$

x	TS_{-1}	TS_{+1}	Difference
1	13	13	0
2	19	19	0
3	22	23	− 1
4	22	25	− 3
5	24	26	− 2
6	25	26	− 1
7	26	26	0

NOTE: T is the sample size.

FIGURE 5.4.   Sample Distributions of the Runs

implies symmetry, whereas the rejection of the hypothesis means that the series is asymmetric in the sense discussed above.

To test the hypothesis displayed in (5.3), we used the Kolmogorov-Smirnov (K-S) statistic D given by

$$D = \max_{x}|S_{-1}(x) - S_{+1}(x)|,$$

where

$S_{-1}(x)$ = the proportion of runs having fewer than x consecutive −1's;
$S_{+1}(x)$ = the proportion of runs having fewer than x consecutive +1's.

Figure 5.4 displays the calculation of this statistic. In this particular case, the sample size is not large enough to reject the null hypothesis since the D

statistic turns out to be .12, whereas a 10 percent significance level yields a threshold of .26. Thus, according to this test, which is fairly conservative (see Gibbons, 1976), the data cannot reject the hypothesis that the sharp drops are a small sample phenomenon.

5.4. BEHAVIOR OF THE AUTOREGRESSIVE REPRESENTATION

Given the low power of the K-S test under the circumstances above, we now investigate the (hypothesized) asymmetry from another angle. We assume that after purging deterministic elements, average labor productivity can be represented by the following qth-order autoregression:

$$X(t) = \sum_{j=1}^{q} \alpha_t(j)X(t-j) + \epsilon(t), \qquad (5.4)$$

where the coefficients obey

$$\alpha_t(j) = \alpha_{t-1}(j) + \xi(t). \qquad (5.5)$$

In other words, we let the autoregressive representation depend on the time parameter t. Further, we assume that the errors $\epsilon(t)$ and $\xi(t)$ are uncorrelated contemporaneously and over time.

Under these conditions, if the behavior of the $X(t)$ series changes during the business cycle, the sequential estimates $[\alpha_t(j)$ for $j = 1, 2, \ldots, t = 3, 4, \ldots]$ would vary periodically and thus would show whether the $X(t)$ series behaves asymmetrically. Using the Kalman Filter, one can easily estimate a system such as in (5.4) through (5.5). Figures 5.4 and 5.6 show these estimates. Figure 5.5 shows the estimate of $\alpha_t(1)$ during the period 1947–1974. Figure 5.6 displays estimates of $\alpha_t(2)$ for the same period. The shaded areas indicate NBER reference cycles. The following can be observed from these estimates: If one does not count the transient behavior for the first few periods, one sees that the estimate of $\alpha_t(1)$ behaves in a fairly stable fashion, whereas the estimate of $\alpha_t(2)$ *does* change significantly before the downturn for almost every recession during the period 1947–1974. Overall, there appears to be a tendency for the $X(t)$ series to become a second-order autoregression a little before the downturns. On the other hand, during the "ups," the $X(t)$ series is closer to being represented by a first-order system. Further, the sum of autoregression coefficients is larger in the case of downturn estimates. Such behavior of $[\alpha_t(j)]$ *is* consistent with the behavior of labor productivity in showing sharp drops but gradual increases.

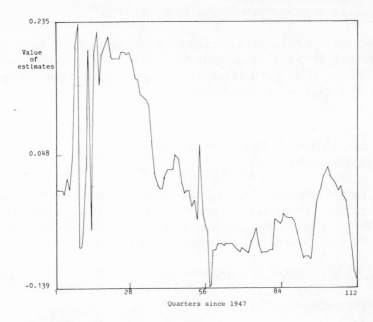

FIGURE 5.5.   Estimates of $[\alpha_t(1)]$

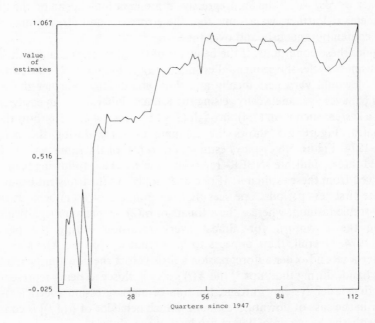

FIGURE 5.6.   Estimates of $[\alpha_t(2)]$

Table 5.1. Estimated Autoregressive Representations

Overall Sample Period

$\hat{X}(t) = 1.06\ X(t-1)\ -\ .13\ X(t-2)$
       $(\ .10)$ $(\ .10)$
$R^2 = .81$

Estimates for Downturn Periods

$\hat{X}(t) = 1.31\ X(t-1) - .33\ X(t-2)$
$R^2\ \ \ = .87$

Estimates for Upturn Periods

$\hat{X}(t) = .87\ X(t-1)\ -\ .001 X(t-2)$
$R^2\ \ \ = .91$

To emphasize this point, we finally estimated the autoregressive system for two different sets of periods. Collecting the data for "downturns" in one subsample, we estimated an autoregressive representation for "downturns," and using the remaining data, we estimated a representation for "upturns." These estimates are shown in Table 5.1. We see that, as argued above, during "downturns" the system is indeed second order, while at other times it is basically a *first*-order representation, with a smaller coefficient. Thus, in the case of upturns, the system adjusts more gradually.

5.5. PREDICTIONS FOR 1975–1978

Finally, the separate autoregressive representations for downturn and upturn periods given in Table 5.1 are used to generate a series of one-step-ahead, out-of-sample predictions of average labor productivity for the period 1975–1978. These predictions are reported in Table 5.2. The same table also contains the predictions obtained from a system that assumes symmetry. According to the mean square error criterion, the "upturn" autoregression does "better" for the years 1975, 1976, and 1977, whereas the system that was estimated assuming symmetry yields better predictions for the year 1978. Thus, the evidence is again mixed: One does not achieve a clear-cut advantage in prediction by assuming asymmetry.

Table 5.2.   Out-of-Sample Forecasts for 1975–1978

		Upturn System		Symmetric System	
	Actual	Prediction	Error	Prediction	Error
1975	− 7.42	− 4.84	− 2.4	− 5.31	− 2.21
	− 5.02	− 6.37	1.35	− 6.96	1.94
	− 2.76	− 4.42	1.66	− 4.37	1.61
	− 4.57	− 2.42	− 2.15	− 2.26	− 2.31
1976	− 3.32	− 4.02	.70	− 4.47	1.15
	− 3.1	− 2.92	− .18	− 2.93	− .17
	− 2.78	− 2.73	− .05	− 2.85	.07
	− 3.35	− 2.44	− .91	− 2.54	− .81
1977	− 3.13	− 2.95	− .18	− 3.19	.06
	− 4.10	− 2.74	− 1.34	− 2.88	− 1.22
	− 2.98	− 3.61	.61	− 3.94	.96
	− 3.36	− 2.62	− .74	− 2.63	− .73
1978	− 5.43	− 2.95	− 2.48	− 3.17	− 2.26
	− 5.61	− 4.78	− .83	− 5.32	− .29
	− 5.18	− 4.94	− .24	− 5.24	.06
	− 5.16	− 4.56	− .60	− 4.74	− .41

5.6.   CONCLUSIONS

In this chapter, we investigated the existence of asymmetry in labor productivity behavior during the business cycle. The results are mixed. A Kolmogorov-Smirnov test applied to the series cannot reject the hypothesis that the observed asymmetry is due to sample variation. On the other hand, a time-varying autoregressive representation for the productivity series suggests that there are systematic shifts in the estimates. Some out-of-sample forecasts presented in the paper also support this view. However, the evidence does not seem to be decisive in either way.

NOTES

1.   There are a variety of reasons behind a delay in laying off workers. First, it may be physically impossible to lower employment instantaneously. Second, if there is uncertainty about the occurrence of a downturn, a producer may lower production, but may still keep the same level of employment until the recession becomes "more certain." Third, workers with "specific training" may never be laid off. A theoretical discussion of these issues is beyond the scope of this paper.

2. Note that the series may "pass" this test, but it may still be asymmetric in some other sense. However, the asymmetry we are dealing with—that is, long stretches of declines but gradual increases—would be detected using this test, given enough observations (see Figure 5.3).

REFERENCES

Bhagwati, J., and R. S. Eckhaus, 1973, eds., *Development and Planning: Essays in Honour of Paul Rosenstein Rodon,* Cambridge, Mass.: MIT Press.

Gibbons, J. D., 1976, *Non-Parametric Methods for Quantitative Analysis,* New York: Holt, Rinehart and Winston.

Gordon, R. J., 1979, "The End-of-Expansion Phenomenon in Short-Run Productivity Behavior," *Brookings Papers on Economic Activity* 2:447–61.

Kuh, E., 1965, "Cyclical and Secular Productivity in United States Manufacturing," *Review of Economics and Statistics.*

Nordhaus, W. D., 1972, "The Recent Productivity Slowdown," *Brookings Papers on Economic Activity* 3:493–536.

Norsworthy, J. R., S. M. Harper, and E. Kunze, 1979, "The Slowdown in Productivity Growth: Analysis of Some Contributing Factors," *Brookings Papers on Economic Activity* 2:387–421.

Oi, W. Y., 1962, "Labor as a Quasi-Fixed Factor," *Journal of Political Economy.*

Sargent, T., 1978, "Estimation of Dynamic Labor Demand Schedules under Rational Expectations," *Journal of Political Economy.*

Sims, C., 1974, "Output and Labor Input in Manufacturing," *Brookings Papers on Economic Activity.*

Solow, R. M., 1973, "Some Evidence on the Short-Run Productivity Puzzle," in Bhagwati and Eckhaus, eds. (1973).

You, J. K., 1979, "Capital Utilization, Productivity, Output Gap," *Review of Economics and Statistics* (February).

III MEASUREMENT ISSUES AND PRODUCTIVITY RELATIONSHIPS

6 TECHNICAL CHANGE, CAPITAL INVESTMENT, AND PRODUCTIVITY IN U.S. METALWORKING INDUSTRIES

Tom Boucher

6.1. INTRODUCTION

Capital investment plays a dual role in the productivity advance of manufacturing industries. It is the means by which human energy is replaced by mechanical power, raising labor productivity at the expense of capital productivity in the interest of minimizing production cost. It is also the vehicle through which new methods of production are absorbed into the capital stock, often creating efficiencies of both capital and labor and resulting in lower unit capital and unit labor costs.

The relative importance of these two roles of capital investment has been addressed by economists in considerable detail. For instance, Brinner (1977) has estimated that over the twenty-five years from 1950 to 1975, capital per man in manufacturing rose at an annual rate of 1.5 percent (cyclically adjusted), while labor productivity increased at 2.6 percent per annum (cyclically adjusted). Under the usual assumptions of perfect competition, con-

The author would like to acknowledge the contribution to this paper provided by the pioneering work of Dr. Lawrence Hackamack in the measurement of machine tool productivity and design change.

stant returns to scale, and neutral technical change, he estimated that increases in capital contributed about .4 percent to the annual expansion in output per man-hour. The remaining 2.2 percent per year was due to "nonquantifiable" components, such as increases in knowledge and efficiency, which include capital-embodied technical change. In other words, by this calculation, the lion's share of productivity advance cannot be accounted for by the increase in an unchanging, hypothetically "pure" stock of capital per worker. Rather, changes in the quality of capital, the education and skills of workers, the organization of work, and scale of production are assumed to account for this residual component. As Solomon Fabricant (1981) has recently pointed out, it is precisely this residual component of productivity advance that has mostly declined in recent years.

The introduction of new methods of production is so completely intertwined with capital investment that a monumental estimation problem presents itself to those who wish to measure the various influences of capital investment on productivity. For example, estimates of the price and quantity of new capital goods are used to measure additions to the capital stock. These estimates are not adjusted for changes in the work capability of individual new capital goods as models change. Over time, design engineers address themselves to the problem of improving the productive capability of capital equipment, and the specific improvements introduced may or may not reflect themselves in proportional increases in equipment price. According to Denison (1974, p. 55), "Improvements in the design of capital goods that raise their net contribution to output are not regarded as representing an increase in capital input (except insofar as they change the cost of a capital good)."

Similarly, modest improvements in the design of new equipment are sometimes adaptable to existing equipment. For example, a manufacturer may retrofit an old machine tool with automatic controls, thereby increasing its productivity at a modest additional cost. A modest price may be paid for more than proportional improvements in the existing stock of capital goods.

There are also problems of capital stock estimation because of shifts in the composition of the stock of capital. Haldi and Whitcomb (1967) investigated the relationship between the purchase price of new "basic industrial equipment" and its output-producing capability from manufacturers' catalogs. They concluded that the productive capability of machines rose much faster than price. A machine costing twice as much usually produced much more than twice the output.

Finally, it is not truly possible to separate the "service" of a machine or unit of capital equipment from its application. That is to say, the services provided by a unit of capital are not homogeneous even for the same machine. In one case, capital equipment may be fully utilized, and in another case, it may be underutilized. In one case, it may be fully utilized in an application that greatly increases productivity, while in another case, it may be fully utilized in a way that provides only marginal improvements in productivity. In fact, it can be argued on economic grounds that the introduction of a piece of capital equipment is most likely to take place in its most productive application, with successive applications less productive. In conventional economic analysis, this problem is subsumed under an assumption of perfect competition, where relative productivity in application is indicated by the marginal return to the input of capital.

Empirical studies of the relationship between capital investment and productivity are of considerable interest to researchers and policymakers. In manufacturing, as in other sectors of the U.S. economy, the general slow-down in productivity advance began in the mid 1960s. As Table 6.1 indicates, output per hour in manufacturing grew at an average rate of 2.8 percent from 1950 to 1965, decreasing to 2.1 percent thereafter. When comparing this to relative levels of capital investment, capital intensity appears to have risen at a much faster rate during the period of slow productivity advance, 1965–1977, rather than during the period of higher productivity advance, 1950–1965. As previously indicated, these measures do not attend to the changing quality of capital and therefore do not provide a very complete assessment of the probable role of capital investment in productivity during these periods.

Table 6.1.   Rates of Change in Output per Hour and Rates of Change in Capital Intensity

| | Annual Growth Rates (percent) | |
	1950–1965	1965–1977
Output per hour		
All manufacturing	2.8	2.1
Nondurable goods	3.2	2.8
Durable goods	2.4	1.6
Capital intensity		
Gross capital per hour	1.7	2.4
Net capital per hour	1.4	2.5

SOURCE: Data on hours and output per hour of all employees were obtained from the Bureau of Labor Statistics. Estimates of the capital stock were obtained from J.C. Musgrave (1976) and the U.S. Department of Commerce (1978).

It is my purpose in the remainder of this chapter to examine the economics of capital investment in one subsector of manufacturing, the metalworking industries. This examination will begin with a review of the recent history of capital investment and productivity advance in these industries. From this will emerge a contradiction that can be explained only by a detailed examination of changes in the design of capital equipment. Direct observations of capital quality in the form of engineering data, which will permit an economic reinterpretation of the results, will be introduced. From this it will be possible to form some general conclusions about the recent history of productivity in these industries and to make some general observations about the future prospects for productivity advance in this subsector of manufacturing.

6.2. CHARACTERISTICS OF THE METALWORKING INDUSTRY

As indicated by Table 6.1, the decline in manufacturing labor productivity after 1965 applies to both nondurable and durable goods industries. The largest portion of durable goods manufacturing is the group of industries engaged in the work of changing the form of metal products through mechanical operations. This class of industries, hereafter referred to as the metalworking industry, will be the focus of this analysis.

The metalworking industry is composed of the following Standard Industrial Classification groups:

SIC 34—fabricated metal products;
SIC 35—machinery, except electrical;
SIC 36—electrical machinery;
SIC 37—transportation equipment;
SIC 38—instruments.

The Standard Industrial Classification system is largely based on some similarity in the industry's end products. For example, the fabricated metal products group produces such items as pipes and valves, plumbing and heating equipment, and metal forgings, while the instruments group produces such products as dental equipment and photographic equipment. Together these industries represent about 40 percent of all manufacturing employment and an equal proportion of value added. Aside from the motor vehicles industry (SIC 371), the group is largely composed of firms organized as job shops; that is, they manufacture discrete parts in small- and medium-sized batches. Over 80 percent of the manufacturing plants in these industries employ less than 100 workers.

A common feature of the metalworking industries is their machine technology base; the tools of production for these industries are mainly provided by the machinery and machine tool manufacturers. For this reason, some portion of the total productivity advance of these industries is associated with advances in the technology of metal cutting and metal forming as it is embodied in the latest machine tool designs. It was with this in mind that such a grouping of industries was chosen for study. It will subsequently be shown that an analysis of quality changes in the machine technology base offers insight into the productivity advance of these industries.

6.3. CAPITAL INVESTMENT AND PRODUCTIVITY ADVANCE IN METALWORKING

Assuming a cost-minimizing management in a two-factor world, the relative prices of capital and labor determine their proportional use in production. As capital goods become less expensive relative to labor and as more capital intense production methods are used, labor productivity rises. It is useful, then, to study the advances of labor productivity with respect to increasing capital intensity. One model for expressing this relationship begins by assuming a Cobb-Douglas production function with constant returns to scale and Hicks-neutral technical change as follows:

$$O_t = A_t L_t^{(1 - b)} K_t^b,$$

where O_t, L_t, and K_t are output, labor, and capital, respectively. A_t is the shift constant, usually referred to as Hicks-neutral technical change, and b is the elasticity of output with respect to capital.

Taking logarithms and differentiating,

$$\frac{\dot{O}}{O} = \frac{\dot{A}}{A} + (1 - b)\frac{\dot{L}}{L} + b\frac{\dot{K}}{K},$$

which, after rearranging, becomes

$$\frac{\dot{O}}{O} - \frac{\dot{L}}{L} = \frac{\dot{A}}{A} + b\left(\frac{\dot{K}}{K} - \frac{\dot{L}}{L}\right).$$

For small changes in output, capital, and labor, the following approximation holds:

$$q^* = a + bk^*, \tag{6.1}$$

where

q^* = the rate of growth in output per man-hour;
k^* = the rate of growth in capital per man;
a = the time shift constant, or technical change.

Table 6.2 summarizes the growth in net capital and net capital per employee for the metalworking industries over three post–World War II subperiods: 1955–1965, 1965–1973, and 1973–1976. With the exception of the last period, these divisions represent peak-to-peak points in manufacturing capacity utilization . Since comparisons are to be made between rates of increase in capital intensity and rates of increase in productivity, it is necessary to avoid confusion of trends with cyclical variations in capacity utilization. The years 1955, 1965, and 1973 are years of approximately the same utilization rate in manufacturing operating capacity.[1] The year 1976 is a year of much lower capacity utilization than the other terminal years; its use is dictated simply by the availability of data pertaining to the capital stock. For that reason, conclusions drawn from the data of this latter period are tentative.

Table 6.2.   Rates of Change in Net Capital and Net Capital per Employee

	Annual Growth Rates (percent)		
	1955–1965	*1965–1973*	*1973–1976*
Fabricated metal products			
Net capital	3.4	4.1	3.6
Net capital per employee	2.2	1.8	6.7
Machinery, except electrical			
Net capital	3.8	5.7	5.3
Net capital per employee	1.9	3.2	5.7
Electrical machinery			
Net capital	5.2	6.9	3.5
Net capital per employee	2.4	4.3	7.2
Transportation equipment			
Net capital	2.7	4.1	3.0
Net capital per employee	2.8	3.7	5.5
Instruments			
Net capital	5.8	7.0	5.3
Net capital per employee	4.2	4.0	4.2
Total metalworking			
Net capital	3.7	5.2	4.0
Net capital per employee	2.3	3.2	6.1

SOURCE: Estimates of the capital stock in 1972 constant dollars were provided from data compiled by the Office of Economic Growth, Bureau of Labor Statistics. Employment estimates are from U.S. Department of Labor (1979).

NOTE: Growth rates were computed using point estimates and the compound growth rate formula.

In most cases displayed in Table 6.2, the characteristic pattern is similar: Rates of growth in net capital are highest during the period 1965–1973 and lower in the preceding and succeeding periods. For the total of all metalworking industries, the characteristic pattern is for a significant increase in the growth rate from the period 1955–1965 to the period 1965–1973, with a significant decrease after the 1965–1973 period.

For the first two periods, growth rates in net capital per employee closely parallel the growth rate of net capital. The unusually large increase in net capital per employee in the 1973–1976 period is in part explained by the fall in capacity utilization from 1973 to 1976 and the incomplete recovery in output and employment levels.

For the periods 1955–1965 and 1965–1973, the overall conclusion is unambiguous. Rates of increase in capital intensity rose from the 1955–1965 period to the 1965–1973 period, reflecting a tendency toward greater substitution of capital in relation to labor during this latter period. Beyond 1973, the data are as yet incomplete. Although growth rates in net capital formation are significantly lower than in the preceding period, this period is generally one of falling capacity utilization, and one would not expect high rates of new net capital formation.

The data concerning rates of growth in capital intensity have implications with respect to labor productivity. Assuming that the rate of technical change is constant, one expects the highest rates of labor productivity growth to correspond with periods of the greatest growth in capital intensity. As shown in Table 6.3, the correspondence does not hold. Across all metalworking industries, labor productivity growth is greatest during the 1955–1965 period, with lower rates in the two latter periods. Once again, the meager productivity growth rates of the 1973–1976 period must be interpreted against the background of falling rates of capacity utilization. However, the comparison between the 1955–1965 and 1965–1973 periods is not subject to such reservation. Despite significantly higher rates of capital intensity in total metalworking during the latter period, the rate of growth in labor productivity displays a significant decrease. Where rates of growth in capital intensity were slightly lower during the 1965–1973 period (fabricated metal products and instruments), the productivity decline is quite dramatic.

In the framework of productivity accounting, the inconsistency between increases in capital intensity and increases in labor productivity is accounted for by shifts in the production function. That is to say, the assumption of a constant rate of technical change cannot be correct; the rate of technical change during the period prior to 1965 must have exceeded that after 1965. Using equation (6.1) as a model, Hicks-neutral technical change was calculated for the three subperiods of interest. As clearly shown in Table 6.4, the

Table 6.3.   Rates of Change in Output per Employee Hour

	Annual Growth Rates (percent)		
	1955-1965	1965-1973	1973-1976
Fabricated metal products	2.2	1.3	0.4
Machinery, except electrical	1.9	1.7	0.3
Electrical machinery	5.1	4.0	1.5
Transportation equipment	2.8	2.3	2.2
Instruments	3.1	2.4	0.8
Total metalworking	2.6	2.2	1.2

SOURCE: Output indexes were provided from the data base compiled by the Bureau of Economic Analysis. Employment and hours for production workers were obtained from U.S. Department of Labor (1979). Man-hours for nonproduction workers are based on a separate estimate prepared by the Bureau of Labor Statistics.
NOTE: Output indexes are based upon estimates of gross product originating in 1972 constant dollars. Growth rates were computed using point estimates and the compound growth rate formula.

assumption of a constant rate of technical change is not defensible. During the period beyond 1965, rates of growth in Hicks-neutral productivity are a fraction of their previous level. Once again, the period beyond 1973 is excused from conclusive analysis because of an incomplete cyclical recovery. However, the comparison between the 1955–1965 and 1965–1973 periods is conclusive.

Table 6.4.   Rates of Change in Hicks-Neutral Technical Change

	Annual Growth Rates (percent)		
	1955-1965	1965-1973	1973-1976
Fabricated metal products	1.8	0.9	− 1.0
Machinery, except electrical	1.5	0.7	− 1.4
Electrical machinery	4.7	2.9	− 0.2
Transportation equipment	1.7	1.1	0.7
Instruments	2.2	1.3	− 1.6
Total metalworking	2.0	1.2	− 0.3

SOURCE: See Tables 6.2 and 6.3.
NOTE: Factor shares were computed from current dollar components of gross product originating provided by the Bureau of Economic Analysis.

Table 6.4 explains the lack of correlation between capital intensity and labor productivity. However, since the data of Table 6.4 are arrived at indirectly (i.e., as a residual), the table does not provide information on the sources of decline in technical change. It would be especially interesting to obtain a more precise understanding of the factors that underlie the presumed shift in the production function. This is the main purpose of the remainder of this paper.

It was stated earlier that a common feature of the metalworking industry is its machine technology base. The interperiod behavior of labor productivity in response to capital intensity, as noted above, is quite characteristic among all the members of this group. Hence, it would seem reasonable to examine the capital-embodied technologies used in this group of industries in an effort to uncover factors that may contribute to the result of Table 6.4.

The next two sections focus on the probable effect of machine design on the observed rates of productivity advance in these industries. In section 6.4, an examination is made of post–World War II trends in machine tool design; section 6.5 offers an economic interpretation of the impact of these design changes on capital investment and productivity advance.

6.4. POST–WORLD WAR II DEVELOPMENTS IN MACHINE TOOL DESIGN

It is the writer's belief that the most pervasive influence on productivity advance is the improvement in design of the tools of production. Furthermore, the reduction in the long-term rate of productivity advance in the metalworking industry can at least in part be attributed to a reduction in the rate at which design innovation has entered the stock of machines. The purpose of this section is to offer evidence in support of this proposition and at the same time to set the stage for an economic interpretation of the relationship between input prices, capital investment, and productivity advance in metalworking.

The period immediately following World War II was one in which many contributions were made to the improved design of conventional machine tools. One major contribution among these improvements was the widespread adoption of carbide cutting tools. Developed in the late 1930s, these tools had the capability of vastly increasing the speed at which metal could be cut, as well as the quantity of metal that could be removed in a single pass. In Table 6.5, some illustrative comparisons are made between carbide and its predecessor, high speed steel, on cutting performance.

Table 6.5.   Representative Cutting Speeds: Carbide and High Speed Steel

| Work Material | Cutting Speed, fpm | |
	High Speed Steel	Carbide
B1112 steel	225	550
1020 steel	180	500
Gray cast iron	110	225
Brass	250	725
Aluminum alloys	300	400
Magnesium alloys	300	700

SOURCE: *Materials and Processes in Manufacturing,* 4/E, by E. Paul De Garmo, Macmillan Publishing Co. Copyright ©, 1974, by Darvic Associates, Inc.

To take complete advantage of this tooling technology, the structural characteristics of the machine required redesign. The ability to perform work at higher speeds and feeds required greater horsepower and more rigid machine construction. In other words, a new generation of machinery had to be built and put into production in order to fully utilize the new tooling technology. Some illustrative statistics on the changing specification of lathes during this period are shown in Table 6.6.

American Machinist magazine estimated that less than 10 percent of the stock of machine tools that existed in 1948 was of current design. At that time, three out of every ten machines in existence had been built in 1938 or before. Six out of every ten machines had been installed between 1939 and 1947, but they were almost entirely of the pre-World War II designs introduced in 1939. These 1939 machines were the first to have the power and

Table 6.6.   Construction and Performance Characteristics of Lathes—1938, 1948, and 1958

	1938	1948	1958
16-inch engine lathe:			
Horsepower	7.5 hp	10.0 hp	20.0 hp
Metal removal rate	16 cu in/min	20 cu in/min	40 cu in/min
RAM-type turret lathe,			
1.5-inch-round stock:			
Horsepower	7.5 hp	10.0 hp	25.0 hp
Weight	3850 lb	4500 lb	5750 lb
Speed	730 rpm	1460 rpm	2000 rpm

SOURCE: *American Machinist,* October 20, 1958.

rigidity to use carbide tooling. The rapid improvements made over these first designs after World War II and the existence of a large stock of machine tools unable to fully utilize such tooling represented a potential for American industry to rapidly increase the productivity of its physical plant by replacing or retrofitting existing equipment.

At the same time, a variety of other important improvements were introduced into conventional machine tools. For example, standardized quick-change tooling systems were developed. Previously, the tool had to be preset in the holder before the holder was mounted on the machine. Subsequently, quick-change toolholders were developed that could be inserted without presetting and the correction made on the machine by adjusting the zero point on the control.

Other innovations that contributed to the productivity of conventional machine tools included automatic gauging and chucking, slide-type machines with box ways to allow heavier cuts, automatic controls, automatic handling in and out, and improved chip breakers. These design advances culminated in the rapid improvement in the production capability of machine tools through the 1950s. Table 6.7 summarizes the magnitude of these improvements by comparing the relative productivity of some new 1958 machine tool types to corresponding new 1948 models. These comparisons, developed by *American Machinist* magazine, represent conservative estimates distilled from data supplied by users of more than 100 different lines of machine tools. These comparisons are largely based on actual job performance of a manufactured product of a given specification. The inescapable conclusion is that the purchase of machinery of 1958 vintage or the retrofitting of

Table 6.7. Productivity of Machine Tools (1958 versus 1948)

Machine	Productivity Factor 1948–1958
Horizontal boring, drilling, and milling	1.75
Vertical boring and vertical turret	2.25
Jig boring	2.00
Broaching	3.70
Engine lathe	1.50
Turret lathe	1.90
Surface grinders	1.55
Bed-type milling machines	2.00
Knee-type milling machines	1.30
Gear hobbing	1.75

SOURCE: *American Machinist,* October 20, 1958.

FIGURE 6.1. Productivity Criteria Quotient for Selected Machine Tools, 1950–1974

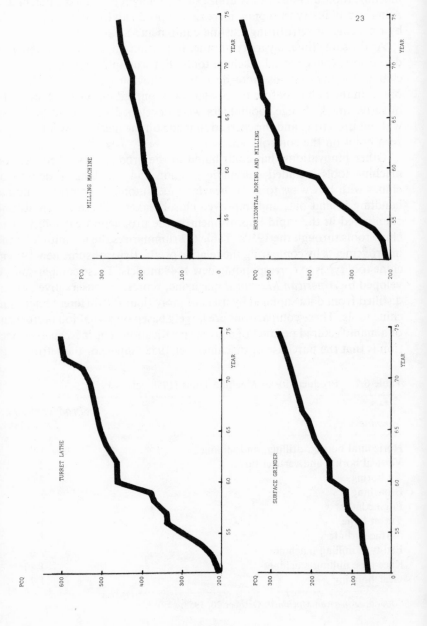

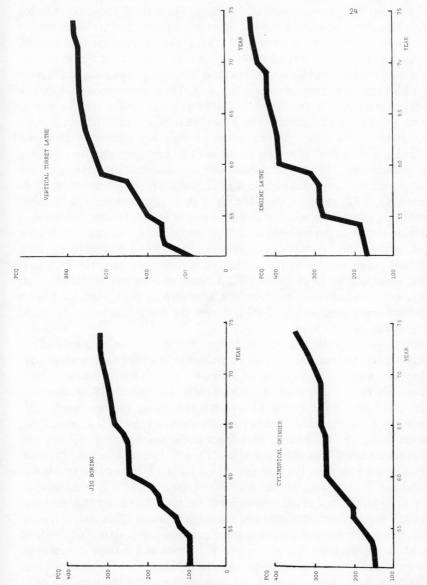

SOURCE: Lawrence Hackamack, Computerized Machine Replacement Service, Inc.

older machines, where possible, represented a great potential for productivity improvement.

The detailed comparisons in Table 6.7 indicate the point-to-point effect of machine design improvements between 1948 and 1958. No comparable data have been developed for the intervening years, nor are there similar data available for the period beyond 1958. However, machine tool productivity data have been developed on a consistent basis by the Computerized Machine Replacement Service (CMRS), a consulting service that advises on machine tool obsolescence and replacement. The machine tool productivity measurement system developed by CMRS is based on the relative importance of changes in machine tool design features and their impact on machine tool productivity over time. When a design improvement is made on a machine tool, it is weighted on the basis of its perceived relative influence on productivity. This weighted time pattern of design improvements is then summarized into an index number series called the productivity criteria quotient (PCQ). For example, the addition of automatic controls on a horizontal boring and milling machine is given a weight of 3 and an improvement in column design is given weight of 2. The numbers are then summed from a base year to yield an index number series that gives a picture of the time path of design improvements introduced into the machine. The PCQ system, developed by Dr. Lawrence Hackamack of Northern Illinois University, was first published by *American Machinist* in 1963. Figure 6.1 is an updated representative set of PCQ curves for some important classes of machine tools.[2]

Since the weighting system is somewhat subjective, the PCQ indexes are only a guide in tracking the rate of change in machine tool productivity. However, a casual examination of Figure 6.1 reveals some common trends among the important classes of machine tools. Through the 1950s, there is a very rapid rate in the introduction of machine design improvements. This agrees with the conclusion drawn from the data of Table 6.7. Beyond 1960, however, the rate of improvement drops as the number of significant new features designed into these machines falls off. Hence, assuming the existence of a lag between the time that a new feature is introduced into a machine and its final incorporation into the capital stock, it is reasonable to suppose that the design improvements of the middle to late 1950s were still being absorbed into the capital stock through the early 1960s. If this is so, it then becomes important to note that the quantum jump in the PCQ scale of most major machines during the late 1950s indicates a large productivity jump over the machines they replaced when these tools were absorbed into the capital stock. In contrast, the machine designs of the 1960s did not offer a similar magnitude of improvement over those of the late 1950s.

This important point is emphasized in Table 6.8. For most major classes of machine tools, the jump in productive capability for the six years prior to 1960 was a multiple of that for the two subsequent six-year periods. Even allowing for large errors in these measures, it seems reasonable to conclude that the strong productivity performance of the metalworking industries through 1965 can at least in part be accounted for by an enormous improvement in the quality of the capital stock. For the period beyond 1965, it is reasonable to assume that the slowdown in the rate of productivity advance is at least in part traceable to much slower rates of change in the introduction of new design features into the capital stock.

Some further indirect evidence in support of this conclusion can be obtained by examining the proportions of capital spending that metalworking firms allocated to modernization during the subperiods of interest. As the stock of machinery ages, deterioration provides a natural incentive to replace worn out equipment. However, assuming a constant rate of deterioration, investment for modernization will proceed more rapidly during periods of rapid machine design improvement. This occurs, of course, because the incentive to modernize is not simply the deterioration of old equipment, but also the absolute difference in economic benefit between the latest machines and those currently in the producer's capital stock. In other words, the incentive to modernize is the combination of deterioration plus technological obsolescence.

As Table 6.9 illustrates, the period 1955–1965 was characterized by greater devotion to the modernization of production facilities than either of the succeeding periods. This is most striking when one considers that the average age of the machine stock at the beginning of this earlier period was far lower than either of the two succeeding periods. In effect, deterioration in

Table 6.8. Absolute Increase in PCQ

	1954–1960	1960–1966	1966–1972
Jig boring	157	41	30
Cylindrical grinder	118	15	34
Surface grinder	74	53	59
Engine lathe	203	29	36
Turret lathe	212	46	87
Horizontal boring and milling machine	230	36	47
Milling machine	118	18	38
Vertical turret lathe	305	71	24

SOURCE: Computerized Machine Replacement Service, Inc.

Table 6.9.   Facility Modernization and Machine Tool Production

	1955–1965	1965–1973	1973–1976
Percent of total capital expenditures on facility modernization and replacement	63	51	52
Percent of machine tool stock			
Less than 10 years old	40	36	33
More than 20 years old	18	23	28
Annual rate of increase (percent) in domestic machine tool production	2.3	– 0.7	– 2.0

SOURCE: Capital expenditures on facility modernization were computed from constant dollar capital expenditure data provided by the Bureau of Labor Statistics, Office of Economic Growth, and estimates of the percentage expended on modernization appearing in the annual McGraw-Hill *Survey of Business' Plans for New Plants and Equipment*. The age of the machine tool stock was compiled by *American Machinist* for the years 1958, 1968, and 1973 and appeared in the following issues: November 17, 1958, November 18, 1968, and October 29, 1973. Increase in domestic machine tool production was computed as the least-squares trend line from data compiled by the Board of Governors of the Federal Reserve system (1977*a*, 1977*b*).

the machine stock through the normal conditions of aging was less of a factor in inducing modernization and replacement during this earlier period. Corresponding to this, the rate of increase in domestic machine tool production was 2.3 percent during 1955–1965, while a decline in production was experienced during the two subsequent cycles.

A summary statement of the likely role of machine tools in accounting for observed rates of technical change is made in Table 6.10, which consolidates some of the critical data previously discussed. Although the net capital stock grew more rapidly after 1965 (line 1), the rate of addition of new vintages of machine tools was falling (line 2). Whatever the composition of the increased capital stock during this later period, it clearly was not accounted for by new metalworking machinery. Finally, the rate of growth in Hicks-neutral productivity (technical change) follows a pattern that is more closely associated with the decline in new machine tools than with the increase in the overall capital stock (line 3). These observations, along with the earlier review of the time path of changes in machine tool productivity, offer some general clues concerning the central role of machinery in transmitting technical change to the capital stock.

Table 6.10. Rates of Change in Capital Formation, Machine Tool Output, and Total Factor Productivity

	Total Metalworking Annual Growth Rates (percent)		
	1955–1965	*1965–1973*	*1973–1976*
Net capital stock	3.7	5.2	4.0
U.S. production of machine tools	2.3	– 0.7	– 2.0
Hicks-neutral productivity	2.0	1.2	– 0.3

SOURCE: See Tables 6.2, 6.4, and 6.9.

The preceding analysis has ignored the role of economic decision making in determining these observed investment patterns. These considerations are developed in the next section.

6.5. THE ECONOMICS OF INVESTMENT IN MACHINE TOOLS

Firms do not purchase machinery simply to increase productivity; the usual objective is to minimize cost. For that reason, it is useful to estimate the economic incentives to invest in machine tools over the periods being analyzed.

The main economic trade-off of interest is that between the price of labor and the price of machine tools. Figure 6.2 illustrates the changing pattern of these prices since 1950. With some variation, the price of machine tools as measured by the wholesale price index has risen at a rate that somewhat parallels that of hourly wages. Machine prices fell off briefly in the early 1970s, but regained upward momentum as energy prices soared, increasing the price of important material inputs, such as iron and steel.

For the periods 1955–1965 and 1965–1973, the net effect of these price movements is summarized in Table 6.11, with an adjustment for investment tax credits. Both machinery and labor prices rose moderately in the late 1950s and early 1960s, but accelerated in the late 1960s and early 1970s. The net effect of these price movements, as indicated on line 3, is approximately the same relative movement in prices during both periods.

Under circumstances of rising relative labor costs, it is usual to expect a pattern of capital acquisition and labor displacement to occur. This is often referred to as the Ricardo effect, since Ricardo was one of the first to dis-

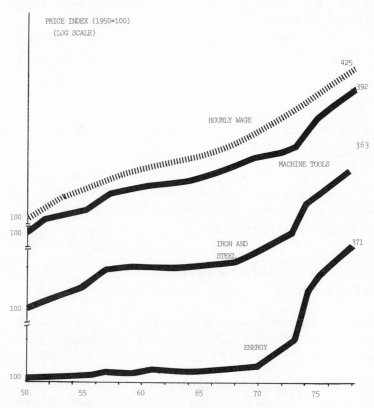

FIGURE 6.2. Metalworking Industries: Prices of Major Inputs

Table 6.11. Movements in Machinery Prices and Labor Wage Rates

| | Percent Change | |
	1955–1965	1965–1973
Machinery prices	25.8	36.6
Labor wage rates	42.2	53.4
Changes in the ratio of labor prices to machinery prices	13.2	12.3

SOURCE: Machinery price data obtained from U.S. Department of Labor (1977). The labor wage for hourly workers in the metalworking industries was computed from data available in U.S. Department of Labor (1976).
NOTE: Machinery prices are adjusted for investment tax credit.

110

cuss it. Since Ricardo, there have been numerous demonstrations of its existence, which no one doubts (see, e.g., Melman, 1956). There has also been discussion concerning the relative importance of the Ricardo effect as compared to the introduction of new methods in production for determining the rate of productivity advance (see, e.g., Salter, 1969). Such discussion is analogous to estimating whether a certain capital investment represents a movement along or a shift in the production function. I will not attempt to enter that discussion here. However, in evaluating changes in machinery prices, the difference between these two effects cannot be ignored.

The machinery price data shown in Figure 6.2 and used in Table 6.11 are taken from the wholesale price index for metalworking machinery and equipment. This index attempts to measure changes in the price of machinery that result from changes in production cost. In accomplishing this task, the market price of a machine is corrected for any changes in machine specification by adjusting the input cost for the specification change. The following is an illustration provided by the Bureau of Labor Statistics (U.S. Department of Labor, 1974):

> The September price for a certain machine used in the calculation of the index was $2,347.50. In October, a new model of the machine was introduced, priced at $2,562.60. The new model was considered essentially comparable with the old, except that it had a more powerful motor and larger tires. These were valued at $186.20 more than the value of those used on the former model. For linking, the September price of the new model was estimated at $2,533.70 ($2,347.50 September price of former model plus $186.20 increase in value of motor and tires). The price comparison between September and October was based on the estimated September price of $2,533.70 and the reported October price of $2,562.60. Thus a 1.1 percent increase was reflected in the October index, but the price change due to quality improvement (more powerful motor and larger tires) was not reflected.

The objective of the WPI is to measure, as closely as possible, pure price changes that result from increases or decreases in the price of a uniform good. In meeting that objective, the series constructed is one that tries to capture the price changes of a hypothetical machine of unchanging specification. As we have seen in section 6.4, such machines do not exist.

To the consumer of machine tools, the relevant price change is not the change in price of a hypothetical machine. Rather, the price of interest is the market price of the actual machine, with the improvements in production capability that are embodied in the new model. It is not inconceivable that, through simplification, the redesign of a machine might reduce its price and improve its functioning. In other words, the buyer is interested in the change in the price of the capital service, which is equivalent to the change in the market price of the machine adjusted for its increased output-producing capability.

If machines of unchanging specification existed, the WPI series would be analogous to a price index of capital services. This would be so because the unchanging machine would have an unchanging output-producing capability, or "service," to provide. Under such conditions, a simple ratio of the change in labor wages to the change in the wholesale price index is indicative of changing relative cost. Even if the rate of technical change were a constant over all periods of time, one could make valid interperiod comparisons of the changing relative price of labor to capital. However, as illustrated in section 6.4, real machines are subject to design changes. In effect, their capital services are increased. In addition, the rate at which these design changes are introduced may vary considerably from period to period. The crucial problem with using the WPI as an index for estimating changes in capital prices is that although it captures changes in production cost, it does not consider the role of design improvements in increasing the quantity of capital services.[3]

With the data provided in section 6.4, it is possible to revise the analysis of Table 6.11 by recasting machine tool prices in terms of the price of a unit of capital service provided by the machine tool. Since the data of section 6.4 are developed on the basis of specific classes of machines, these revised estimates of the changing relative cost of capital and labor will be performed on the same basis for machine tools on which data are available. Only the results will be presented, but a comprehensive description of the manner in which the data were developed is contained in the appendix of this chapter.

Table 6.12 summarizes the results obtained by recalculating machinery prices on a capital service basis. The choice of periods was determined by the availability of machinery price data. For the eight machine types surveyed, which comprised about a third of metal-cutting machine tool shipments in 1963, the incentive to substitute capital for labor was much greater in the period of the late 1950s and early 1960s than in succeeding years. Based on an average weighted by 1963 sales, the change in labor prices relative to the price of capital services in the earlier period was over three times that of the latter period. Even allowing for fairly large errors of measurement in the data, the result would seem to be consistent with a general incentive to modernize production facilities in the late 1950s and early 1960s. In addition, it is reasonable to infer that the greater output-producing capability of the newer models over those that they replaced explains in part the more rapid rate of increase in total factor productivity over the 1955–1965 period.

Table 6.12. Changes in the Ratio of the Price of Labor to the Price of Capital Services by Major Machine Type

	Percent Change	
	1954-1963	1963-1972
Engine lathe	69	14
Turret lathe	71	23
Vertical turret lathe	95	9
Horizontal boring and milling	39	7
Milling machine	58	17
Jig boring	51	24
Cylindrical grinders	58	22
Surface grinders	101	47
Weighted average	64	20

SOURCE: See chapter appendix.

6.6. THE CURRENT PERIOD

The increase in energy prices since 1973 has affected the capital substitution process in two respects. First, it has directly increased the cost of running a machine by raising the unit power bill. In the metalworking industries, as opposed to most process industries, this is still a small portion of unit cost. More important, though, has been the indirect effect of increasing the cost of material inputs used in the manufacture of machines, such as steel, which consume large quantities of energy in production.

Table 6.13 provides a summary of price changes in specific classes of machines since 1973. In the absence of available data on machine design improvements over this period, no firm conclusions can be drawn. However, since the price of machinery has outstripped the price of labor through this period, significant improvements in machine tool productivity are required to offset unfavorable production cost movements and to effect real capital service price reductions.

6.6.1. The Role of Numerical Control and Computer-Aided Manufacturing

The previous description of technical change in machine tool design focused on conventional machine tools. A major unconventional machine tool innovation of the last twenty years is the numerically controlled (NC) machine.

Table 6.13.   Increases in the Wholesale Price Index, 1973–1977

	Percent Increase
Conventional machines	
Boring mill, vertical	48
Cylindrical grinding machines	57
Rotary surface grinding machines	59
Engine lathes, 16-inch swing or under	64
Milling machines	46
Numerical control	
Boring, drilling, and milling machines, NC	61
Jig borer, NC	89
Turning machine, NC	49
Multifunction machines, NC	34
Metalworking machinery and equipment, total	58
Labor wage rate	39

SOURCE: U.S. Department of Labor (1974, 1978).
NOTE: NC indicates numerically controlled.

Numerical control does not imply a different kind of machine; rather, it is a technique for controlling a machine. An NC machine is a basic machine tool equipped with a controller programmed to decode instructions fed to the machine to control its operations. The more sophisticated controllers are equipped with sensing devices that transmit machine status back to the control unit. This closed-loop feedback enables the controller to verify that the machine operation conforms to the input instructions.

This study has not explicitly dealt with the impact of numerical control on machine tool productivity; however, this omission was not crucial. Over the major periods of interest in this study, 1955–1965 and 1965–1973, numerical control was a negligible factor. Of the 2.6 million machine tools in the capital stock in 1978, only an estimated fifty thousand were numerically controlled. In effect, the absence of data on NC machines does not significantly influence the results previously presented.

With regard to any prognosis of future productivity trends in metalworking, an understanding of the economics of numerical control and computer-aided manufacturing is important. Table 6.13 has given some indication of the relatively rapid price inflation of conventional machine tools. With the current outlook of continued high price inflation in energy and raw materials, there is every reason to believe that the price of the basic machine is likely to continue its strong upward climb. On the other hand, part of the price structure of an NC machine is the price of the controller. With present advances in the manufacture of large-scale integrated circuits driving the cost of computer components down, the controller has actually become less expensive. The interaction of these economic forces, as well as the future potential application of numerical control and computer-aided manufacturing methods to the metalworking industry, is not yet fully diagnosed. Table 6.13 indicates that, with the exception of multifunction machines, price increases of numerically controlled machine tools have not fared much better than those of conventional machines over the period 1973–1977. However, it has been estimated than NC machines reduce part cycle time from 20 to 75 percent (*American Machinist,* October 16, 1972). Hence, it is not possible to make inferences about the economic importance of numerical control from relative price increase data alone.

6.6.2. The Present Age of the Capital Stock

Another important factor in the current period is the age of the existing machine tool stock. In 1978, about 69 percent of the machine tools in the capital stock were ten years old or over, and 34 percent were twenty years old or older. As I pointed out earlier, even in the absence of technical change, one economic incentive for machine replacement is deterioration through wear and tear. At no time in the post–World War II period has the average vintage of existing machines been so antique. In the absence of data on the functional deterioration of older machine tools, it seems reasonable to expect that some machine replacement will be stimulated simply in the interest of discarding worn-out equipment.

6.7. SUMMARY

Capital investment plays a dual role in improving labor productivity. First, through the substitution of mechanical energy for human energy, labor productivity can be increased at the expense of capital productivity. Second, capital investment is the medium through which embodied technical change is realized in production, often resulting in both labor and capital productivity improvements.

These dual roles of capital investment have been examined for a large segment of the manufacturing sector—the metalworking industries. It was shown that the significant slowdown in labor productivity since the mid 1960s does not correspond to a slowdown in aggregate capital substitution.

Rates of growth in capital per employee were greater for the period beyond 1965 than for the period up to 1965. Instead, the evidence presented indicates the existence of a strong complementarity between productivity and improvements in the quality of machinery used in production by the firms of these industries. The higher rates of improvement in machine tool technology before 1960 and their subsequent absorption into the capital stock complement the observed increase in the residual component of labor productivity. It is concluded that the differential rate of change in this residual, Hicks-neutral technical change, is in part explained by the complementary differential rates of change in machine tool design improvements.

In this chapter, I have made no attempt to attribute a portion of the movement of total factor productivity to the technical change embodied in machinery. Such a growth-accounting exercise is beyond the scope of the data presented here. My purpose has been simply to enliven some interest in research on the role played by current capital formation in the introduction of technological change. It is that portion of productivity advance that is attributable to technical change that has historically been the largest component and is now most rapidly decreasing.

I hope the observations made in this study stimulate research on a number of important, related questions. First, what are the circumstances surrounding the time path of technical innovation in conventional machine tools? It was pointed out earlier that the introduction of carbide tooling was a major factor in the post–World War II rapid productivity increase. Ceramic tools, which followed carbides, had the potential to again greatly increase cutting speeds, but they were not widely used because of their lack of toughness and tendency to fracture. However, cutting time is not the only productivity-related variable in machine design; the amount of time a conventional machine tool is cutting metal is only a portion of total cycle time. Setting up and breaking down work pieces before and after machining consumes a large portion of total work time in most job shops. To some extent, this fact was influential in the development of multifunction NC machines on which multiple cutting operations can be performed, thus eliminating the need for multiple setups on separate machines. One open research issue is to determine what economic and other factors have influenced the direction of development work on conventional machine tool design since the 1950s.

A second question, closely related to the first, concerns the assessment of current technological innovations in machine design. If we assume that long-term energy and raw-material price inflation is a fact of life for the 1980s, it is clear that the historical pattern of labor productivity increase achieved by replacing manpower with horsepower has arrived at difficult times. In a world of rapidly rising energy prices, the economic incentives for this direct substitution process are coming to a halt, if not reversing. For these reasons, economists interested in technical change should be assessing the economics of computer control, which some members of the scientific and engineering community believe to be the new vehicle for continuing the substitution process, in this case by displacing manual materials-handling and decision-making functions with computer control. Currently, advanced research in this area includes the development of machine vision (computer optics) for the identification and handling of components by robots; computer language for geometric identification and modeling; and unmanned, computer-aided systems of metalworking machine tools (called flexible manufacturing).[4]

An integral part of assessing the future economic importance of these emerging manufacturing methods is a consideration of the manufacturing environment within which this technology must operate. Automation and computer aids in manufacturing have historically been first introduced in process industries, such as petroleum, chemicals, and pharmaceuticals. These industries are characterized by long production runs of a relatively homogeneous product, for which a science-based model (called a chemical synthesis) exists. Traditional discrete-parts manufacturing (the job shop) has none of these advantages. Hence, there exist difficult problems of systems modeling, production scheduling, and production control, for which appropriate computer software must be developed. An important adjunct to the economic evaluation of emerging hardware developments in discrete-parts manufacturing is an understanding of the existing organization of production and its influence on the potential use of such hardware.

Finally, I hope the methods of analysis used in this study stimulate research on the effects of machine-embodied innovation on machine productivity. Today, a large number of industrial processes are essentially machine-paced; that is, the speed of production is in large measure built into the design of the equipment. Examples of this exist in the canning, electronics, steel, cement, pulp mill, and tobacco industries, as well as a number of other industries. In these cases, it is almost impossible to imagine productivity advance realized from technical change without new net capital formation. It should also be appreciated that the productivity-inducing effects of different kinds of capital formation may differ markedly: computers versus machine tools, materials-handling equipment versus pollution control equipment. In addition, there is no reason to believe that one is correct in constructing models that assume that constant rates of embodied technical change characterize capital formation; the evidence of section 6.4 refutes this entirely. These facts and the current interest in understanding and accounting for the unexplained residual component of productivity advance are strong incentives for theoretical and empirical work on the measurement and determinants of embodied technical change. Hence, a useful improvement in our knowledge about productivity advance may be achieved by focusing our attention more directly on the tools of production—a joint endeavor for both the economic and engineering professions.

APPENDIX: SOURCES AND METHODS OF TABLE 6.12

In computing the ratio of labor prices to capital service prices, the labor wage series for the various metalworking industries was compiled from data of the Bureau of Labor Statistics (see U.S. Department of Labor, 1976).

The price of capital services was computed by taking an index of machinery prices by machine and adjusting it for changes in the output-producing capability, or "service," provided by the machine. The resulting index indicates the changing price of the service.

Machine Price Data. The first step is to obtain data on the change in machinery prices, but for the reasons explained in the text, the wholesale price index of metalworking machinery prices is not an appropriate place to begin. Ideally, one would like to obtain market prices for machinery, to which one could make an adjustment for productivity as between vintages. The only publicly available price data that serve this purpose are the unit price relative data of the *Census of Manufactures*. The census unit values are based on the quantity and value of shipments figures published for individual products. For example, quantity and shipments data are collected for engine lathes (SIC 354152) by swing diameter as follows: up to and including 16 inch (SIC 3541521); 17 inch to 23 inch (SIC 3541523); 24 inch to 36 inch (SIC 3541525); over 36 inch (SIC 3541529). The relative change in the unit values between census years is based on product shipments and is not adjusted for specification changes. Unfortunately, except for the products that are highly specified, unit values may be subject to changes due to changes in product mix. However, these deflators have the advantage of reflecting actual transaction prices at the level desired—f.o.b. plant level. Census unit value relatives can be computed using the data of Table 6A of the *Census of Manufactures*, vol. 2. Aggregations at the five-digit level are published in *Indexes of Production*, vol. 4, of the *Census of Manufactures*.

In section 6.5, the comparison of changing labor to machinery prices was made between the census years 1954–1963 and 1963–1972. Census unit price relatives were used in estimating the change of machinery prices in the

1954–1963 period. With the exception of lathes, the BLS wholesale price indexes at the five-digit level were used for the 1963–1972 period. This was done principally because the change in unit price relatives for the machine tools of interest seemed unusually high during this latter period. This may have been the result of an unusual change in product mix. Since the purpose of the exercise is to contrast the order of magnitude of the change in labor to capital prices between the two periods of interest, the BLS deflator, which understates the actual prices paid for new models, was used in this latter period. This is justified on two counts. First, it is better to bias the comparison in favor of the 1963–1972 period. In so doing, the larger increase of the labor to capital price ratio in the earlier period is more convincing. Second, if design changes did not proceed at a rapid rate during the latter period, adjusted BLS price data are not likely to be very much lower than the actual unadjusted price changes. BLS price relatives were taken from *Indexes of Production,* vol. 4, of the *Census of Manufactures.*

Machine Productivity Data.   The data presented in section 6.4 were used as the basis for computing machine productivity changes. The engineering data of Table 6.7 were linked with the PCQ series of Figure 6.1. For each machine, the ratio of the percent productivity improvement from the period 1948–1958 to the number of PCQ unit increases during that period was used to extrapolate productivity improvements by machine to 1972. This is clearly a rough procedure and is largely dependent on how accurately PCQ curves mirror productivity change.

Calculation of Relative Price Change.   The procedure used to combine price and productivity changes can be illustrated as follows:

Milling Machine

	Percent Change	
	1954–1963	*1963–1972*
Increase in machinery price	30.3	50.0
Increase in machine productivity	48.1	14.9
Increase in price of capital service	− 12.0	30.5
Increase in labor wage rate	39.1	53.2
Increase in the ratio of labor prices to the price of capital services	58.1	17.4

NOTE: For the period 1954–1963, the increase in the price of capital service = $[(1.303 \div 1.481) - 1] \times 100$, and the increase in the ratio of labor prices to the price of capital services = $[(1.391 \div .88) - 1] \times 100$.

NOTES

1. Annual average capacity utilization in manufacturing for 1955, 1965, and 1973 was 87.0 percent, 89.6 percent, and 87.6 percent, respectively.
2. The PCQ system of productivity measurement is presently applied to fifty-seven classes of machine tools, including numerical control. It has been used by private companies as a planning tool in capital investment and productivity improvement, allowing a firm to assess the potential for replacing machines based on differences in capabilities between vintages. The representative machine tool groups used in this study are those for which a PCQ series has been compiled back to 1939 and for which data have previously been published. See, for example, the following issues of *American Machinist:* November 11, 1963; June 7, 1965; October 7, 1968.
3. An associated question that should be raised concerns improvements in the labor force, or labor services. Lacking any quantitative information about the time path of changing skill levels among machinery operators, the assumption of a constant rate of change is made.
4. For a partial summary of the research currently going on in this area, as sponsored by the National Science Foundation (NSF), see *Seventh NSF Grantees' Conference on Production Research and Technology* (NSF, 1979).

REFERENCES

American Machinist, October 20, 1958, "Plan 59," Special Report No. 466.
_____, November 17, 1958, "The 8th American Machinist Inventory of Metalworking Equipment."
_____, November 11, 1963, "Productivity, How Do Your Machines Rate?"
_____, June 7, 1965, "PCQ, Spotting Productivity Change."
_____, October 7, 1968, "PCQ, New Machine Ratings."
_____, November 18, 1968, "The 10th American Machinist Inventory of Metalworking Equipment."
_____, October 16, 1972, "NC for Profit and Productivity."
_____, October 29, 1973, "The 11th American Machinist Inventory of Metalworking Equipment."
Board of Governors of the Federal Reserve System, 1977*a*, *Industrial Production,* 1976 revision, Washington, D.C.: U.S. Government Printing Office.
_____, 1977*b*, *Industrial Production Indexes, 1976,* Washington, D.C.: U.S. Government Printing Office.
Brinner, R. E., 1977, "Manufacturing Productivity Growth, Capital Formation and Policy—Outlook and Options to 1990," in National Center for Productivity and Quality of Working Life (1977).
DeGarmo, E. P., 1974, *Materials and Processes in Manufacturing,* New York: Macmillan.
Denison, E. F., 1974, *Accounting for U.S. Economic Growth, 1929-1969,* Washington, D.C.: Brookings.
Dogramaci, A., ed., 1981, *Productivity Analysis: A Range of Perspectives,* Boston: Martinus Nijhoff Publishing.

Fabricant, Solomon, 1981, "Issues in Productivity Measurement and Analysis," in Dogramaci, ed. (1981).

Haldi, J., and D. Whitcomb, 1967, "Economics of Scale in Industrial Plants," *Journal of Political Economy* 75 (August).

McGraw-Hill, various years, *Survey of Business' Plans for New Plants and Equipment,* New York: McGraw-Hill.

Melman, S., 1956, *Dynamic Factors in Industrial Productivity,* Oxford: Basil Blackwell.

Musgrave, J. C., 1976, "Fixed Nonresidential Business and Residential Capital in the United States, 1925-75," *Survey of Current Business* (April).

National Center for Productivity and Quality of Working Life (NCPQWL), 1977, *The Future of Productivity,* Washington, D.C.: NCPQWL.

National Science Foundation (NSF), 1979, *Seventh NSF Grantees' Conference on Production Research and Technology,* Ithaca, N.Y., September 25-27.

Salter, W. E. G., 1969, *Productivity and Technical Change,* Cambridge: Cambridge University Press.

Shapiro, E., 1970, *Macroeconomic Analysis,* New York: Harcourt, Brace, and World.

U.S. Department of Commerce, *Census of Manufactures,* Washington, D.C.: U.S. Government Printing Office.

U.S. Department of Commerce, Bureau of Economic Analysis, 1978, "Fixed Nonresidential Business and Residential Capital in the United States, 1975-77," *Survey of Current Business,* April.

U.S. Department of Labor, Bureau of Labor Statistics, 1974, *Annual Supplement to the 1974 Wholesale Prices and Price Indexes,* Washington, D.C.: U.S. Government Printing Office.

_____, 1976, *Employment and Earnings,* Bulletin 1312-10, Washington, D.C.: U.S. Government Printing Office.

_____, 1977, *The Handbook of Labor Statistics,* Washington, D.C.: U.S. Government Printing Office.

_____, 1978, *Annual Supplement to the 1978 Producer Prices and Price Indexes,* Washington, D.C.: U.S. Government Printing Office.

_____, 1979, *Employment and Earnings,* Bulletin 1312-11, Washington, D.C.: U.S. Government Printing Office.

7 THE ROLE OF CAPITAL FORMATION IN THE RECENT SLOWDOWN IN PRODUCTIVITY GROWTH

J. R. Norsworthy and Michael J. Harper

7.1. OVERVIEW

This chapter examines the role of capital formation in the slowdown after 1965 in labor productivity growth in the nonfarm business sector from about 3 percent per year to less than 2 percent per year. The rate of capital formation is found to have had no role in the slowdown in the 1965-1973 period and a significant role in the 1973-1977 period. However, pending investment data revisions and incomplete recovery from cyclical movements in 1974 and 1975 make the latter conclusion tentative. The findings are compared with those of the Council of Economic Advisers, the Council on Wage and Price Stability, and others who have reported a significant role for capital. The chief cause for the difference in findings is misalignment of the capital stock measures with the output and labor input for the nonfarm business sector. When this misalignment is corrected, the rate of capital formation and its influence on labor productivity growth are shown to be essentially unchanged from the earlier periods of 1948-1955 and 1955-1965.

As part of the analysis the appropriate method for aggregating the components of the capital stock is investigated. Direct aggregation—based on the maintained hypothesis of a Cobb-Douglas production function—is

122

found to be unjustified based on econometric tests. Translog or Divisia aggregation of the capital stock components—based on the maintained hypothesis of a translog production function, a more general functional form—is found to be justified; that is, the test for weak separability of capital asset types from the labor input passes, while the test for strong separability fails.

Capital productivity is found to have declined during the 1965–1973 and 1973–1977 periods after rising in the earlier periods. Time series on prices of capital, labor, and energy inputs—in the light of the findings of other investigators that capital and energy are complementary in production—suggest stronger substitution of capital for labor in the 1965–1973 period and much weaker substitution in the 1973–1977 period.

Appendix A of this chapter describes the econometric tests for aggregation. Appendix B examines the sensitivity of the findings to investment for pollution abatement. The findings are not changed.

7.2. CAPITAL FORMATION IN THE NONFARM BUSINESS SECTOR

Labor productivity growth in the private sector of the U.S. economy received a considerable boost between the end of World War II and the mid-1960s because of the relative (as well as absolute) shift of labor from the farm to the nonfarm sector. In 1947, about 20 percent of the U.S. private labor force was engaged in agriculture; by the mid 1960s, the proportion had fallen to about 5 percent.[1] For this reason, analysis of possible contributing factors to slowdown in labor productivity growth is perhaps best carried out in abstraction from this shift.[2] The nonfarm business sector, which excludes production by nonprofit institutions and private households, is the largest nonfarm aggregate sector for which the Bureau of Labor Statistics (BLS) publishes quarterly and annual measures of labor productivity. It is this sector that has been most closely analyzed by Clark (1977, 1978), the Council of Economic Advisers (1978), and the Council on Wage and Price Stability (1978) in their approaches to explaining the productivity slowdown. It is important to exclude the nonprofit and household sectors because their output is measured by labor input in the national income and product (or GNP) accounts, which provide the framework for aggregate output and capital and labor input measures. The BLS labor productivity measures also include government enterprises; that is, activities of federal, state, and local governments selling services directly to the private sector. Because capital measures for these activities are not compiled, government enterprises are excluded from the nonfarm business sector for the purpose of our analysis. The exclusion of this small sector—about 2.4 percent of employment in nonfarm business—has minimal effect on the pattern of labor productivity growth. Thus, the analysis of the effect of capital formation for the sector is likewise minimally affected.

Common to the capital stock measures used by Clark, the Council of Economic Advisers (CEA), and the Council on Wage and Price Stability (CWPS) in discussing the labor productivity slowdown in the nonfarm business sector is a misalignment of the capital stock with the output and labor input measures from which labor productivity is computed. Their investigations used the stock of private nonresidential capital compiled by the Bureau of Economic Analysis (BEA). This measure of the capital stock differs from the appropriate measure for the nonfarm business sector in two important respects: The capital stock of equipment and structures of nonprofit institutions are included in the Clark-CEA-CWPS measure, and the stock of tenant-occupied residential capital is excluded. Because the output and labor input for nonprofit institutions are excluded from the nonfarm business sector, the associated capital stock should also be removed. Similarly, because the output and labor input for tenant-occupied housing are included in the target sector, the associated capital stock should also be included. As Table 7.1 clearly shows, these differences significantly change the growth profile of the net stock of equipment and structures. Each difference tends to reduce the average annual rate of growth in the two earlier periods and to raise it in the later period. This misalignment of the capital stock measure with the measures of output and labor input significantly affects the conclusions about the comparative growth of the capital stock and hence the capital/labor ratio in the earlier and later time periods since 1947. Thus, Table 7.1 shows the net capital stock of equipment and structures in the nonfarm business sector to be growing about 20 percent faster in the 1965–1973 period rather than slowing somewhat.

To assess the relationship between capital formation and the growth of labor productivity, a temporal framework is required. In analyzing the same problem, based on quarterly data, Clark (1978, p. 2) argues as follows:

> One simple method for disentangling trend productivity growth from cyclical variations is to pick time periods that are judged to be at the same stage in the business cycle and then calculate the growth rate between these periods. These "peak to peak" growth rates contain only trend terms and random disturbances, and are relatively free of cyclical components.

Because we agree with Clark's reasoning and also for comparability with his results, we have selected the same time periods for analysis.[3] We analyze

Table 7.1. Reconciliation of Nonresidential Business Capital Growth to Business Capital Growth—Nonfarm Sector, Net Stocks, 1972 Dollars, and Average Annual Rates of Change

	Nonresidential Business Capital, Private Nonfarm	− Capital of Nonprofit Institutions	= Nonresidential Capital, Private Business	+ Tenant-Occupied Private Capital	= Nonfarm Business Capital (Equipment and Structures Only)	+ Landlord Inventories	= Nonfarm Business Capital Only
	*	*	*	*	*	*	*
1948	304.41	25.23	279.18	128.42	407.60	158.11	575.71
	4.05	5.69	3.88	1.19	3.14	3.03	3.10
1965	597.08	64.67	532.41	156.73	689.14	261.09	950.23
	4.79	4.02	4.88	2.93	4.45	4.05	4.34
1973	867.47	88.58	778.88	197.46	976.34	358.47	1334.81
	2.61	0.95	2.80	0.31	2.31	1.38	2.05
1977	961.60	92.01	869.59	199.90	1069.49	378.11	1447.60

SOURCE: Basic data from the Bureau of Economic Analysis.
NOTE: *indicates annual rate of change.

125

the problem in terms of average annual rates of change for the following periods: 1948–1955, 1955–1965, 1965–1973, and 1973–1977. Our focus is on the contrast between the 1965–1973 period and the two earlier periods. Data for the 1973–1977 period are reported, but they must weigh less heavily in the analysis for two reasons. First, the year 1977 is clearly not a peak either for the business cycle or—based on the evidence of the first three quarters of 1978—for labor productivity. Second, and perhaps most important, the dramatic change in the trend of energy prices that began in late 1973 appears to have changed the historic pattern of substitution between capital and labor. In particular, while our analytic framework examines only capital and labor, work by other investigators—notably Berndt and Wood (1975) and Hudson and Jorgenson (1978*a*, 1978*b*)—shows complementarity between capital and energy inputs. Consequently, a sharp increase in the price of energy would be expected, ceteris paribus, to decrease the rate of growth of the capital stock.[4]

7.3. MEASUREMENT OF CAPITAL INPUT

An additional issue influencing measurement of the growth of the capital stock is whether net or gross capital stocks of equipment and structures should be used. Clearly, for productivity analysis, it is real capital input that must be the target concept. The appropriate question thus is whether net or gross capital stock—or indeed some other measure—is the better indicator of real input. In accounting terms, the difference between the gross and net capital asset measures is the accumulated depreciation on the asset. The method of depreciation and the service life of the capital asset are the determinants of depreciation. There is precedent for using gross capital stock, several varieties of net capital stock, and a linear combination of the two. We have not attempted here to resolve the issue; we have opted for the net measure (as do the preponderance of other productivity analysts) as being somewhat better. There is evidence that the results are not sensitive to the choice of measures: The net stock of equipment and structures in the nonfarm business sector grew at an average annual rate of 3.1 percent in the 1948–1965 period and 4.4 percent in the 1965–1973 period; the gross stock grew at rates of 2.7 percent and 3.9 percent in the respective periods. The changes in the rates of growth therefore differ by only one-tenth of 1 percent.

Cyclical adjustment of the variables entering an analysis of productivity growth is full of pitfalls. Investigations by Mohr (1980) and Nadiri and Rosen (1973) have conclusively demonstrated that adjustments of input factors to patterns of output movements are strongly interrelated and described by a matrix of adjustment coefficients.

Consequently, the adjustment process among just three input factors—say, equipment, structures, and labor—is described by nine lagged adjustment coefficients. These findings lead us to reject any attempt to adjust for cyclical effects beyond choosing comparable peaks in the business cycle. Gollop and Jorgenson (1980) and Kendrick (1973, 1976), for example, make no cyclical adjustment in the capital input. Clark (1978, pp. 3–4) adjusts labor productivity directly for cyclical movements in a way that leaves the peaks largely unchanged. He also adjusts the labor input in his capital labor ratio by the index of capacity utilization for manufacturing (1977, p. 11).[5]

Competing techniques for aggregation of the capital stock and of inputs in general have figured prominently in the discussion of productivity analysis in recent years. Perhaps the issue is most clearly stated in the broader debate between Denison and Jorgenson and Griliches.[6] In simplest terms, the issue turns on whether the constant dollar values of assets comprising the capital stock should be added directly—direct aggregation, practiced by Denison and Kendrick—or whether an index of capital input should be computed as the weighted sum of the growth rates of the individual assets, using the shares of each asset type in total capital compensation as weights. The latter method, elaborated below, is variously called a Divisia, Tornqvist, or translog index.[7] In econometric terms, the validity of direct aggregation results in an exact index for the maintained hypothesis of a Cobb-Douglas production function, which entails strong separability of the various factor inputs. The translog index, as we shall call it, results in an exact index under the maintained hypothesis of the far more general homothetic translog (from transcendental logarithmic) production function, which entails weak separability of factor inputs and which subsumes the Cobb-Douglas form as a special case. We have performed econometric tests for weak and strong separability of the capital and labor inputs for the nonfarm business sector. The test for weak separability passes by a wide margin; that for strong separability fails decisively. The testing procedures and results are reported in detail in Appendix A of this chapter. In the analysis that follows, therefore, the results based on translog aggregation of the capital input should be given considerably more weight than those based on direct aggregation, although both techniques are used. In particular, the failure of the econometric test for strong separability of the capital input from labor implies that we cannot make inferences from the level of the capital stock—or the level of the capital/labor ratio. The success of the test for weak separability implies that we can make valid inferences from the growth rates of these quantities.

In measuring total real capital input for productivity analysis, it is conventional to include not only measures of equipment and structures, but of land and inventories as well. Stocks of inventories measured in current and constant dollars and adjusted for price changes are reported by the Bureau of Economic Analysis, again in the framework of the GNP accounts. Corresponding measures of land input are not available from that source. Kendrick (1973) has estimated the input of land for the nonfarm business sector, and we have adopted his measures.

There are other dimensions, however, to the inclusion of inventories in the capital stock for productivity analysis. While it is clear from our conventional conception of economic progress how plant, equipment, and land augment the labor input and hence that an increase in the capital labor ratio should, ceteris paribus, lead to higher labor productivity, the function of inventories seems comparatively obscure. It can even be argued that inventories have no function whatever in the model of pure competition and instantaneous factor adjustment that underlie the neoclassical theory of productivity measurement and analysis.

With regard to the latter point, we rely for the purposes of this analysis on our choice of peak periods in the business cycle to give comparable inventory-to-output ratios. We suppose that there is some direct, if unspecified, usefulness of inventories in the production process and thus include inventories as part of the real capital stock.[8] In this practice, we do not differ from other productivity analysts—Denison (1974), Gollop and Jorgenson (1980), and Kendrick (1973)—except perhaps in acknowledging the potential problem involved.

7.4. AGGREGATION OF THE ELEMENTS OF THE CAPITAL STOCK

Direct aggregation of the components of the capital stock for some year t consists of simply adding the components measured in constant dollars as follows:

$$K_t = E_t + S_t + L_t + I_t,$$

where E, S, L, and I denote the net stocks of equipment, structures, land, and inventories, respectively. The growth of capital input is then defined as follows:

$$\frac{\dot{K_t} = (K_t - K_{t-1})}{K_{t-1}},$$

where $\dot{K_t}$ represents the growth rate in capital input for year t.

Translog (or Divisia or Tornqvist—see note 7) aggregation consists in adding the growth rates of the asset types of the capital stock weighted by the respective shares, w_a, of each asset type in nonlabor payments (or total property income). Thus, the rate of growth of capital input is obtained directly as follows:

$$\dot{K}_t = w_E \dot{E}_t + w_S \dot{S}_t + w_L \dot{L}_t + w_I \dot{I}_t,$$

where

$$\sum_a w_a = 1,$$

for $a = E, S, L, I$.

The shares of each component in nonlabor payments for a given sector of the economy are determined as follows (subscripts denoting time are omitted for readability):

$$w_a = R_a Q_a,$$
$$R_a = (rP_a Y + \delta_a P_a - \Delta P_a)Z_a + TP_a,$$

where

R_a = the rental price of asset a;
Q_a = the constant dollar quantity of input of asset type a;
r = the internal rate of return;
P_a = the investment price deflator for asset a;
ΔP_a = the change in P_a from the previous period;
Y = the product of the corporate tax rate and the ratio of equity to debt plus equity;
δ_a = the rate of depreciation for asset a;
Z_a = an allowance for the tax deductibility of payments to the asset;
T = an allowance for property taxes.

This approach to measuring the service price of capital assets follows that of Christensen and Jorgenson (1970). However, we did not make a separate calculation as they did for corporate and noncorporate enterprises; we assumed that the price of capital services for each asset type is the same in the noncorporate sector as in the corporate sector. The depreciation term is zero for both land and inventories. The series from BEA for inventories include reevaluation for price change. This measure of capital price was applied for the manufacturing and nonfarm, nonmanufacturing sectors within nonfarm business. Specific internal rates of return and ratios of equity to debt plus equity were determined for each sector, and the aggregation was performed across both sectors, using shares for each asset type for each sector in total nonlabor payments for the nonfarm business sector. Based on this translog aggregation and the unweighted aggregate, we can define the effect of changes in asset type and changes in the sectoral distribution of capital assets.[9] For any one year (or span of years), we define the total effect, $\dot{q}_K$, of changes in the composition of the capital stock as follows:

$$\dot{q}_K = \dot{K} - \dot{K}_o,$$

where $\dot{K}$ is the growth rate of the weighted capital aggregate and $\dot{K}_o$ is the growth rate of the unweighted capital aggregate. We can partition $\dot{q}_K$ by constructing a partial translog aggregate $\dot{K}_m$ by adding growth rates across the manufacturing and nonfarm, nonmanufacturing sectors (with assets within sectors aggregated directly), using the shares of each sector in nonlabor payments for nonfarm business as weights. Similarly, we construct a partial aggregate $\dot{K}_A$ of growth rates across asset types (with asset types aggregated directly across sectors) weighted by shares of each asset type in nonlabor payments for nonfarm business. In this case, the capital service prices are computed for the nonfarm business sector as a whole and used to compute asset shares. Then the intersectoral "shift effect," or contribution to growth in the capital stock from changes only in sectoral shares of the total capital stock, can be defined as follows:

$$\dot{q}_M = \dot{K}_M - \dot{K}_o.$$

The "asset effect," or contribution to growth in the capital stock from changes in only the asset composition of the capital stock, can be defined as follows:

$$\dot{q}_A = \dot{K}_A - \dot{K}_o.$$

In general, it will not be the case that the interindustry shift effect, $\dot{q}_M$, and the asset effect, $\dot{q}_A$, exactly exhaust the total composition effect, $\dot{q}_K$, on the growth rate of the capital stock; that is, there may be some (generally quite small) interaction effect that can be computed as follows:

$$\dot{q}_I = \dot{q}_K - \dot{q}_M - \dot{q}_A.$$

As Table 7.2 shows, the differences in resulting growth rates between direct and translog aggregations of the capital stock are not large, but they do change the pattern of annual growth rates between the first two time periods from acceleration in capital formation to a slight slowdown, while the acceleration in growth from the second to the third period is increased. This

Table 7.2.   Average Annual Growth Rates of Capital Stock—Nonfarm Business Sector, for Direct and Translog Aggregations of Equipment, Structures, Land, and Inventories

	Direct Aggregation	Translog Aggregation	Total Composition Effect $\dot{q}_K$	Asset Effect $\dot{q}_A$	Inter-sectoral Shift Effect $\dot{q}_M$	Inter-action Asset and Shift $\dot{q}_I$
1948–1955	3.00	3.33	0.33	0.22	0.08	0.03
1955–1965	3.24	3.19	− 0.05	− 0.01	− 0.08	0.04
1965–1973	4.30	4.56	0.26	0.24	0.0	0.02
1973–1977	2.04	2.18	0.14	0.18	0.0	− 0.04

latter effect is important because it is the role of capital formation in labor productivity growth in the 1965–1973 period that is primarily at issue.

As comparison with Table 7.1 shows, the effect on the growth rate of the directly aggregated capital stock attributable to inclusion of land and inventories is to reduce the rates of growth somewhat in the first two periods and to raise the growth rate slightly in the third. There is a sharp contrast between the patterns of capital growth rates for nonfarm, nonresidential business—which excludes land and inventories and is aggregated directly—and for the nonfarm business sector based on translog aggregation. Rather clearly, however, the major factor contributing to the difference is the misalignment of the capital stock with the definition of the nonfarm business sector.

The composition effect in the capital stock is dominated by the asset effect in three of the four periods studied; the net effect over all four periods of the intersectoral shift effect is very nearly zero. Because only two sectors are included, this small effect is not surprising. By contrast, Gollop and Jorgenson (1980) find a larger shift effect and a correspondingly smaller asset effect in a system encompassing fifty-one industries.[10] A probable explanation for this difference is that industry is functioning as a proxy for differences in asset types, particularly equipment, which are reflected in differences in movements of equipment price deflators among industries.[11] Thus, ceteris paribus, shifts in the intersectoral distribution of the capital stock will reflect wider price differences than for the aggregated measures presented here.

7.5. GROWTH OF THE CAPITAL/LABOR RATIO

In appraising the effect of capital formation of labor productivity, it is useful to discuss the growth of the capital/labor ratio to link the descriptive measures of growth of the capital stock and the more inferential quantitative assessment of the contribution of capital formation to growth in labor productivity. The capital/labor ratio is a familiar shorthand method for describing the capital intensiveness of production. One of the major limitations to its usefulness—the failure of the capital/labor ratio to distinguish among asset types—is partially overcome in translog aggregation of growth rates because the growth rates of assets of different values—reflecting different marginal productivities—are commensurately reflected in the growth rate of the aggregate capital stock. Table 7.3 shows the growth rates of the capital/labor ratio for the four time periods for both direct and translog aggregations of the capital stock. The denominator for the measure—hours for all persons engaged in the nonfarm business sector—is the same as for the labor/productivity ratio, output per hour of labor input.[12] Growth rates are shown for aggregates based on equipment and structures only, as well as for all four asset types, for comparability with the earlier analyses by Clark, CEA, and CWPS. The results are unambiguous: There is no slowdown in the growth of the capital/labor ratio in the nonfarm business sector for the 1965–1973 period, regardless of the method of aggregation or the range of the assets included in the capital stock. Consequently, based entirely on descriptive methods rather than more subtle econometric inference, the proposition that a slowdown in growth of the capital stock contributed to the decline in labor productivity in the 1965–1973 period is refuted. And, just as clearly, there has been a slowdown in the growth of the capital/labor ratio since 1973 of more than 1 percent per year. (However, as noted above, 1977 is not comparable to the earlier peaks in business activity.)

Table 7.3. Average Annual Growth Rates of the Capital/Labor Ratio—Nonfarm Business Sector, for Direct and Translog Capital Aggregates

	Direct Aggregation		Translog Aggregation	
	ES	ESLI	ES	ESLI
1948–1955	2.00	1.96	2.21	2.29
1955–1965	2.28	2.31	2.15	2.26
1965–1973	2.53	2.38	2.64	2.64
1973–1977	1.46	1.31	1.51	1.45

NOTE: ES indicates equipment and structures only; ESLI indicates equipment, structures, land, and inventories.

7.6. THE LINK BETWEEN CAPITAL FORMATION
AND LABOR PRODUCTIVITY

While our discussion to this point has been largely descriptive in nature, any causal link between the rate of capital formation and the rate of labor productivity growth is necessarily inferential and therefore subject to a wider range of interpretation. To estimate the impact of the growth of the capital stock on labor productivity, we adopt the Jorgenson framework.[13] Except with respect to the presumed form of the production function and the pricing of capital services, whose effects are captured in the composition term $\dot{q}_K$ as noted above, the Jorgenson analytic framework depends on the same maintained hypotheses about the nature of economic activity as those of Denison and Kendrick: The prices of inputs are equal to their marginal productivities; the underlying production process is homogeneous with respect to input quantities.[14]

The simple expression for measurement of Hicks-neutral productivity change in a competitive equilibrium is

$$\dot{A} = \dot{O} - w_K \dot{K} - w_L \dot{L},$$

where

$\dot{A}$ = Hicks-neutral productivity change;
$\dot{O}$ = growth in real output—measured as the value added by capital and labor;
w_K = capital's share in the current dollar measure of output;
w_L = labor's share in current dollar output;
$\dot{L}$ = the growth in labor input;
$\dot{K}$ = the growth in real capital input.

Rearranging algebraically, we obtain

$$\dot{O} - \dot{L} = w_K(\dot{K} - \dot{L}) + \dot{A}.$$

For small changes, $\dot{O} - \dot{L} = (\dot{O}/L)$ and $\dot{K} - \dot{L} = (\dot{K}/L)$; that is, the change in labor productivity can be expressed as Hicks-neutral productivity change plus the change in the capital/labor ratio weighted by capital's share. The effects of change in the composition of the capital stock and of the labor force can be inferred as well. Recalling $\dot{K} = \dot{K}_o + \dot{q}_K$, we can analogously define $\dot{L} = \dot{L}_o + \dot{q}_L$, where $\dot{q}_L$ represents the (total) effect of composition changes in the labor force.[15] We can then express labor productivity—measured as output per unit (hour) of directly aggregated labor input, partitioned into contributions from (1) changes in the capital/labor ratio based on directly aggregated capital and labor, (2) changes in the composition of the capital stock,[16] (3) shifts in the interindustry allocation of labor, and (4) Hicks-neutral technical change. The last term is clearly a residual, the measure of our ignorance in this particular analysis. (Recall that the objective is to measure the effect of capital formation, not to explain as fully as possible the sources of productivity growth.) Algebraically, we can express the measurable contributions to labor productivity growth in the final framework

$$\left(\frac{\dot{O}}{L_o}\right) = w_K\left(\frac{\dot{K}_o}{L_o}\right) + w_K\,\dot{q}_K + w_L\,\dot{q}_L + \dot{A}\cdot$$

The results of this partitioning are shown in Table 7.4, based on the full measure of real capital input, including equipment, structures, land, and inventories. All elements of the capital stock are included because capital's share—in the current dollar value of output nonlabor payments—includes the returns to all real assets. As would be anticipated from the growth pattern of the capital/labor ratio, the effect of the capital stock on labor productivity increased in the 1965–1973 period as compared with the earlier periods. Significantly, direct aggregation and translog aggregation give different results for the comparative contributions of capital in the first two periods: Rather than a larger effect in the 1955–1965 period, as one would infer using direct aggregation (incorrectly, as we have noted above), capital formation in that period actually contributed somewhat less than in the 1948–1955 period. The increase in the impact of capital formation is larger for the 1965–1973 period as compared to earlier periods when translog aggregation is used. However, the conclusion is not changed by the method of aggregation. Intersectoral shifts in labor have minimal effects in the first three periods. The major source of the slowdown in labor productivity growth is in the other factors whose effects are captured in the Hicks-neutral or residual terms.[17]

Although the evidence for the 1973–1977 period is not comparable for the reasons noted above, there is an entirely different pattern in this period: The effect of capital formation declines almost by half, and the labor shift contributes negatively to labor productivity growth. Indeed, more of the slowdown from the 1965–1973 period to the 1973–1977 period is explained than is left in the residual term: Of a decline in growth of 0.87 percent per year, 0.52 percent is explained by our analysis. Therefore, based on the maintained hypotheses underlying this productivity accounting framework, far from exerting a drag on labor productivity growth in the 1965–1973 period, capital formation actually contributed somewhat more than in the earlier postwar periods.

Table 7.4. Effect of Net Capital Stock and Other Factors on Labor Productivity Growth in the Nonfarm Business Sector

	Labor Productivity Growth $(\dot{O}/L_o)$	Effect of Changes in				Total Effect of Capital Stock $W_K(\dot{K}/L_o)$
		Capital/ Labor Ratio $w_K(\dot{K}_o/L_o)$	Composition of Capital Stock $w_K\dot{q}_K$	Intersectoral Allocation of Labor $w_L\dot{q}_L$	Other Factors $\dot{A}$	
1948–1955	3.00	0.66	0.12	0.02	2.20	0.78
1955–1965	2.80	0.76	− 0.01	− 0.03	2.08	0.75
1965–1973	1.96	0.80	0.09	− 0.01	1.08	0.89
1973–1977	1.09	0.41	0.05	− 0.09	.72	0.46

7.7. CAPITAL PRODUCTIVITY MOVEMENTS

The measure of capital productivity that is analogous to labor productivity as measured by the BLS for major sectors of the economy is simply output per unit of real capital input. Few investigators have appraised this measure to any degree, although Kendrick (1976) is an exception. Table 7.5 shows the average annual rates of growth in capital productivity in the nonfarm business sector measured in this way for the same time periods that we analyzed earlier. In this instance, there is a striking contrast between the earlier two periods and the later two periods: Capital productivity first rises and then declines. Once again, the results are not sensitive to the choice of aggregation method, although the patterns of growth differ noticeably. When based on direct aggregation, capital productivity growth falls sharply from the first to the second period, whereas the decline is moderate for translog aggregation. The reason for this reversal is not to be found in differential rates of output growth; output grew 3.88 percent per year in the 1965–1973 period, almost exactly the average rate for the two earlier periods combined. Furthermore, in the 1973–1977 period, output grew at less than half its earlier rate, and yet the rate of the capital productivity decline was slightly more than half that in the 1965–1973 period.[18]

A partial explanation may be found in conventional economic terms—price-induced substitution of capital for labor. In the 1948–1955 period, the price of labor grew 1.65 percent per year faster than the price of capital services; in the 1955–1965 period, 2.15 percent faster; in the 1965–1973 period, 4.21 percent faster; and in the 1973–1977 period, 0.98 percent faster. In other terms, these differences measure the relative price change of labor as compared to capital. The price incentive to substitute capital for labor was thus about twice as strong in the 1965–1973 period as compared with the earlier periods. A factor retarding the increase in the price of capital services—which differs from the price of additions to the capital stock by inclusion of tax effects—is the investment tax credit for equipment that went into effect in the mid 1960s. While we have at present no measures of the elasticity of substitution between capital and labor that would permit direct appraisal of these price changes, one could readily construct a comparative statics diagrammatic or mathematical example wherein optimal adjustment to relative price change implies substitution of capital for labor to such an extent that capital productivity falls, even in the presence of positive Hicks-neutral technical change. A more meaningful approach, however, would be to estimate the production function in a form that permits testing of this hypothesis. To date, we have not done so, and our explanation is therefore conjectural.

Table 7.5. Average Annual Rates of Growth in the Nonfarm Business Sector—Capital Productivity, Output, and Prices

	Capital Productivity (Direct Aggregation) $(\dot{O}/K_o)$	Capital Productivity (Translog Aggregation) $(\dot{O}/K_o)$	Output $\dot{O}$	Price of Capital Services	Labor Compensation per Hour	Price of Energy Inputs
1948–1955	1.03	0.70	4.03	3.51	5.17	0.09
1955–1965	0.49	0.54	3.73	2.27	4.42	0.45
1965–1973	− 0.43	− 0.68	3.88	2.27	6.48	3.17
1973–1977	− 0.23	− 0.37	1.81	8.05	9.03	25.32

NOTE: As regards price of energy inputs, because energy prices rose in late 1973 in consequence of the oil embargo, the average price increase for the 1965–1972 period was extended to 1973. The resulting price level for 1973 was used as the basis for computing the average rate of increase from 1973 through 1977. It is doubtful that investment decisions based on late 1973 energy prices significantly affected the net capital stock at year end. The series for energy prices is the wholesale price index for fuels and related products and electric power.

If the relative price explanation for the decline in capital productivity is correct for the 1965–1973 period, one would expect different results in the 1973–1977 period, when the relative price change was so small. Aside from the incompatibility of this period with the earlier ones in terms of cyclical movements and data reliability, there is another major factor involved: the dramatic surge in energy prices that took place in late 1973 and early 1974.

Complementarity between capital and energy has been found by Berndt and Wood (1975) and by Hudson and Jorgenson (1978b). Consequently, it may be argued that the sharp rise in energy prices made a significant part of the capital stock economically obsolete. If so, real capital input grew more slowly from 1973 to 1977 than the estimates indicate—and thus contributed even more to the productivity growth slowdown than is indicated in Table 7.5—because more of investment was directed toward replacement of the existing capital stock than is measured by the conventional depreciation formulas used by the Bureau of Economic Analysis. Of course, this explanation is conjectural.

Finally, there is the rapid and continued rise in employment since the trough of the recession in the first quarter of 1975. This phenomenon, which has been widely noticed and described as puzzling, is somewhat more understandable in light of (1) the complementarity between capital and energy and the increase in energy prices, and (2) the much closer movement in the prices of capital and labor. Increases in output under these conditions would be achieved with relatively greater expansion of labor input and less of capital (and hence energy) than under the price that has prevailed since 1948, in general, and in the 1965–1973 period in particular. These were the findings outlined in Hudson and Jorgenson (1978a).

7.8. CONCLUSIONS

A real slowdown in labor productivity growth occurred in the nonfarm business sector in the period 1965–1973. However, during this period, the growth of real capital input accelerated, as did the growth of the capital/labor ratio and the contribution of the capital stock to labor productivity growth. Therefore, we conclude that capital formation did not contribute to the slowdown in labor productivity growth. The conclusion is not sensitive to the method of aggregation of the capital stock. The translog index of capital growth—for which the associated econometric test passes—shows faster growth of the capital stock than does the direct aggregation index—for which the associated econometric test fails. The patterns of growth shown by the two aggregation methods do differ significantly, however. The conclusion is sensitive to proper alignment of the capital stock measure with output and labor input for the nonfarm business sector. Improper alignment is directly responsible for the contradictory results reported by Clark, CEA, and CWPS.

The slowdown in labor productivity growth from 1973 to 1977 is clearly associated with a decline in growth of the capital/labor ratio, which is possibly attributable to the sharp increase in energy prices.

Capital productivity rose in the 1948–1955 and 1955–1965 periods and declined thereafter. The decline in the 1965–1973 period may be associated with the rise in the price of labor as compared with the price of capital services. These last two propositions can best be appraised in econometric analyses that include the adjustment of input factor demand to changes in output levels and input factor prices, especially energy prices since 1973.

APPENDIX A: SEPARABILITY TESTS WITH THE TRANSLOG PRODUCTION FUNCTION

For testing the hypothesis of Hicks-neutral technical change, a translog production function with factor-augmenting technical change was used.[19] This function, termed structure A, including output (Q), labor (L), capital (K), and time (t), is as follows:

$$\ln Q = \alpha + \beta_L \ln L + \beta_k \ln K + \beta_t t + \gamma_{LK} \ln L \ln K$$

$$+ \frac{1}{2} \gamma_{LL} \ln^2 L + \frac{1}{2} \gamma_{KK} \ln^2 K + \gamma_{Lt} t \ln L$$

$$+ \gamma_{Kt} t \ln K + \frac{1}{2} \gamma_{tt} t^2.$$

Imposing $\beta_L + \beta_k = 1$, and $\Sigma_i \gamma_{ij} = 0$, for all j, and estimating the share equations, the model becomes

$$ML = \beta_L + \gamma_{LL}(\ln L - \ln K) + \gamma_{Lt} \cdot t$$
$$ADA = \beta_t + \gamma_{Lt}(\ln L - \ln K) + \gamma_{tt} \cdot t.$$

Here ML is the share of labor compensation and ADA is the growth rate of output minus the growth rate of the translog index of capital and labor. These equations arise from taking $(\partial \ln Q)/(\partial \ln L)$, $(\partial \ln Q)/(\partial \ln K)$, and $(\partial \ln Q)/(\partial t)$, and imposing the parameter restrictions.

We are required to drop $(\partial \ln Q)/(\partial \ln K)$ from the estimating system since its parameters can be derived directly from those of $(\partial \ln Q)/(\partial \ln L)$ using the restrictions. The left-hand sides arise as follows: By definition, $(\partial \ln Q)/(\partial \ln L) = (\partial Q/\partial L)(L/Q)$. By imposing the assumption of competitive factor markets (a necessary condition for efficient production), $P_L = (\partial Q)/(\partial L)$, we can replace $(\partial \ln Q)/(\partial \ln L)$ with ML, labor's share. ADA is a discrete approximation to the rate of change of output with respect to time, $(\partial \ln Q)/(\partial t)$.

The test for Hicks-neutral technical change consists of imposing $\gamma_{Lt} = 0$ (no bias in technical change), which is equivalent to the test for separability. Weak separability involves imposing $\gamma_{Lt} = \rho \beta_L$ and $\gamma_{Kt} = \rho \beta_K$, while strong separability requires $\rho = 0$.[20] Note that each appears to impose one parameter restriction (eliminate one parameter). However, since $\gamma_{Lt} = -\gamma_{Kt}$, then $\rho \beta_L = -\rho \beta_K = -\rho(1 - \beta_L)$. Since $\beta_L \neq \beta_L - 1$, ρ must be 0. Thus, strong separability requires weak separability, as well as that $\gamma_{Lt} = -\gamma_{Kt} = 0$; that is, no bias in technical change.

The test statistic was generated as follows: The parameters were estimated using the iterative Zellner method.[21] The estimated variance-covariance matrix of the untransformed disturbances, $\Sigma \hat{\Omega}$ was retrieved. The weighting matrix, W (for transforming the above matrix), was retrieved; the parameters were reestimated with the restriction imposed and with W held constant. The new variance-covariance matrix, $\Sigma \hat{\omega}$, was retrieved. The following statistic is then chi-squared with one degree of freedom (presuming the restriction represents no significant simplification):[22]

$$n \text{ trace } (\Sigma \hat{\Omega}^{-1} \Sigma \hat{\omega} - n),$$

where n is the number of degrees of freedom.

Based on data from the national income and product accounts and coordinate measures of labor and land inputs, this test was performed for five sectors: manufacturing; nonfarm nonmanufacturing; farm; private business (which is the sum of the first three sectors); and nonfarm business (which is the sum of the first two). The results are summarized in Table 7.6. The data are the Divisia index of capital over asset types, the Divisia index of labor input over relevant one-digit sectors, and current dollar output. The estimates of γ_{Lt}, γ_{tt}, and γ_{LL} presented are from the unconstrained model. The negative signs of γ_{tt} reflect the productivity slowdown. The imposition of $\gamma_{Lt} = 0$ generates significant chi-squared values (3.84 at the 5 percent significance level) for each of the disaggregate sectors and insignificant ones for private business and nonfarm business. This apparently occurs because γ_{Lt} has opposite signs in manufacturing ($-.0029$) and nonfarm nonmanufacturing ($.0051$).

In structure A, β_L is the share of labor; $(1 - \beta_L)$ the share of capital; $-\{(\gamma_{LL})/[\beta_L(1 - \beta_L)]\}$ the elasticity of substitution of labor for capital; γ_{Lt} the bias of technical change toward labor augmentation; and γ_{tt} the rate of change of the rate of technical change.

Table 7.6. Parameters from the Factor Augmentation Model and Test for Hicks-Neutral Technical Change

	γ_{Lt}	γ_{tt}	$\sigma_{KL} = (\gamma_{LL})/[\beta_L(1-\beta_L)]$	Chi-Square for Hicks-Neutral Test (reject over 3.84)
Private business	−.0019 (.0025)	−.00056 (.00040)	.42 (.33)	1.17
Farm	−.023 (.012)	−.0021 (.0014)	1.20 (.86)	7.46
Nonfarm business	.00073 (.00211)	−.00043 (.00041)	−.0003 (.088)	.26
Nonfarm nonmanufacturing	.0051 (.0013)	−.00042 (.00034)	−.046 (.012)	33.98
Manufacturing	−.0029 (.0014)	−.00031 (.00077)	.044 (.012)	9.61

NOTE: As regards column 3, it is possible to compute the test for the elasticity of substitution at each data point; that is, for each time period. Such a test would be based on substituting the observed labor shares M_{Lt} for β_L (the estimated labor shares over the whole period). We chose the approach reported here as more appropriate for the whole time period under consideration.

141

Structure B begins with the following production function:

$$\ln Q = \alpha + \beta_L \ln L + \beta_{K1} \ln K1 + \beta_{K2} \ln K2 + \gamma_{LK1} \ln L \ln K1$$

$$+ \gamma_{LK2} \ln L \ln K2 + \gamma_{K1K2} \ln K1 \ln K2$$

$$+ \frac{1}{2} \gamma_{LL} \ln^2 L + \frac{1}{2} \gamma_{K1K1} \ln^2 K1 + \frac{1}{2} \gamma_{K2K2} \ln^2 K2.$$

Imposing $\beta_L + \beta_{K1} + \beta_{K2} = 1$ and $\Sigma_i \gamma_{ij} = 0$, for all j, the estimated equations are:

$$ML = \beta_L + \gamma_{LL}(\ln L - \ln K_2) + \gamma LK_1(\ln K_1 - \ln K_2),$$
$$MK_1 = \beta_{K1} + \gamma_{LK1}(\ln L - \ln K_2) + \gamma_{K1K1}(\ln K_1 - \ln K_2).$$

Structure B was applied to four sets of capital assets as follows:

$B1$: K_1 = translog index of structures, inventories, and land;
    K_2 = equipment;
$B2$: K_1 = translog index of inventories and land;
    K_2 = translog index of equipment and structures;
$B3$: K_1 = translog index of structures and land;
    K_2 = translog index of equipment and inventories;
$B4$: K_1 = equipment;
    K_2 = structures;
    Q = value added less compensation-paid inventories and land.

In structure B, weak separability involves imposing $\gamma_{LK1} = \rho\beta_{K1}$ and $\gamma_{LK2} = \rho\beta_{K2}$. The chi-squared test is the same as the one performed for structure A. In this case, the second run is performed on the share equations with these restrictions imposed. Strong separability was tested by the t-statistic associated with ρ in the second run. Significance of 5 percent was split equally between the weak and strong test.[23] The relevant chi-square and t cutoff values were 5.02 and 2.00, respectively. Table 7.7 summarizes the results. In most cases, the data confirm the translog index (chi-squared test) for combining capital assets while rejecting direct aggregation (t-test).

APPENDIX B: THE EFFECT OF POLLUTION CONTROL INVESTMENT ON THE GROWTH OF CAPITAL STOCK

The Bureau of Economic Analysis has collected data since 1973 on capital expenditures for pollution control. The methodology for their survey is reported by Cremeans (1974, 1977). McGraw-Hill, in its survey of capital

Table 7.7.   Separability of Assets

Type of Separability Sector	Weak Separability (reject for chi-square > 5.02) Chi-Square	Strong Separability (reject for t > 2.00) t	
Eq from *Sr* + *La* + *Iy*			
Private business	.26	2.83	reject
Farm	3.39	8.92	reject
Nonfarm business	2.60	3.53	reject
Nonfarm nonmanufacturing	8.31 reject	1.55	meaningless
Manufacturing	31.57 reject	5.18	meaningless
Eq + *Sr* from *La* + *Iy*			
Private business	.17	2.75	reject
Farm	1.70	7.58	reject
Nonfarm business	.07	3.49	reject
Nonfarm nonmanufacturing	8.60 reject	1.79	meaningless
Manufacturing	25.95 reject	4.91	meaningless
Eq + *Iy* from *La* + *Sr*			
Private business	2.98	2.85	reject
Farm	.38	4.29	reject
Nonfarm business	5.64 reject	3.41	meaningless
Nonfarm nonmanufacturing	4.93	1.45	
Manufacturing	.29	6.33	reject
Eq from *Sr*			
Private business	.002	.78	
Farm	.011	8.42	reject
Nonfarm business	.57	1.78	
Nonfarm nonmanufacturing	2.82	2.08	reject
Manufacturing	.33	2.10	reject

expenditures, has collected such data since 1968 (McGraw-Hill Book Company, Economics Department). The BEA survey clearly defines pollution control expenditures, while the McGraw-Hill survey does not; consequently, total control expenditures in the McGraw-Hill survey are substantially higher than in the BEA survey. The rates of change from the McGraw-Hill survey have been used in Vaccara (1975) to extrapolate the BEA 1973 expenditure level back to 1968. Prior to 1968, there are no consistent data available on which to base estimates of the capital stock associated with pollution control expenditures; consequently, "considerable ingenuity" is required to deduce the differential effect from the periods 1947–1955 and 1955–1965 to the 1965–1973 period.

For this reason, we have concluded that the quality of time series that could be constructed is too poor for inclusion in the analysis reported in the text. Rather, we test the sensitivity of our results to worst-case assumptions about the possible effects. The CWPS (1978, Table III-4, p. 49) estimates that the growth rate of the net capital stock of equipment and structures was reduced by 0.3 percent in the 1967–1973 period by pollution control expenditures. If we assume no effect in the earlier periods—surely the limiting case—and weight this change by the average share of equipment and structures in the total capital stock (equipment, structures, land, and inventories) for the 1965–1973 period, we obtain a maximum effect of 0.21 percent per year on the growth rate of the capital stock. This effect is then weighted by capital's share in current dollar output to obtain 0.06 percent per year, the negative effect on labor productivity growth in the framework represented in Table 7.4. Thus, pollution control expenditures would reduce the contribution to labor productivity growth of growth in the capital/labor ratio from 0.80 percent per year to 0.74 percent per year. The total effect of capital formation in the 1965–1973 period (including composition changes —based on translog aggregation) would then be 0.83 percent per year, compared with 0.75 percent per year from 1955 to 1965 and 0.78 percent per year from 1948 to 1955. Consequently, the most extreme assumptions about the effects of pollution abatement investment do not alter the conclusion that the rate of capital formation played no role in the slowdown in productivity growth in the 1965–1973 period.

When more data become available, it will be possible to estimate the role of pollution abatement expenditures on capital formation by contrasting the data with the data from the period since 1973. Denison (1978) has examined the effect of all pollution abatement expenditures (labor as well as capital), as well as the effect of health and safety and crime control expenditures, on productivity growth for the 1968–1975 period and finds substantial contributions to the productivity slowdown from these sources.

NOTES

1. The impact of this reallocation is discussed in Norsworthy and Fulco (1974) and need not be repeated here.

2. By analyzing productivity growth for this sector, we also sidestep the issue of whether the farm-to-nonfarm shift effect should be considered part of the "reallocation of resources" as a source of output and productivity growth, as in Denison (1974), or part of the change in labor force composition, as in Gollop and Jorgenson (1980).

3. Because the Bureau of Economic Analysis publishes only annual capital stock data, the quarterly dimension of a capital stock series for the nonfarm business sector is somewhat dubious. In addition, the lag between capital investment and actual engagement of the new

capital in the production process would render the quarterly data somewhat suspect even if data were collected and published on that basis.

4.   The capital data for the years 1975–1977 are also less reliable. Measures of real investment in equipment and structures for these years were revised upward in July 1978. As of this writing (October 1978), these upward revisions have not been incorporated into the measures of capital stock, and current plans at the Bureau of Economic Analysis are to do so only in early 1979.

5.   The implication of these two simultaneous adjustments for the form of the production function is not easy to deduce. In any event, because output is more volatile in this manufacturing sector than in the nonfarm business sector as a whole, Clark's method is likely to "overadjust."

6.   The debate, which originated in the *Review of Economic Studies*, is presented with further remarks by the participants in a supplement to the *Survey of Current Business* on the measurement of productivity, May 1972.

7.   While a rose by any other name would smell as sweet, terminology in economics sometimes leads to substantive confusion. The Divisia index, properly speaking, is a continuous index (see Jorgenson and Griliches, 1967), and some of the superior mathematical properties claimed in justifying its use occur only in its continuous form. Its application in productivity analysis necessarily involves a discrete approximation to the continuous Divisia form, because inputs and outputs are measured only at discrete points in time, not continuously. The particular approximation to the Divisia index used by Jorgenson and his associates was independently derived by Tornqvist (1936). Because the index we use is based on the maintained hypothesis of a translog production function, we use the term *translog index* and refer to the associated aggregation technique as *translog aggregation*.

8.   One may posit a simple model of the production process with an explicit role for inventories as follows:

$$S_t = g(P_t, I_t);$$
$$P_t = f(K_t, L_t);$$
$$I_{t+1} = P_t - S_t + I_t,$$

where

t = the current time period;
I_t = current inventories;
P_t = current output;
S_t = current shipments;
K_t = current real capital stock;
L_t = current labor input;

and where all are measured in real units.

In this model the firm (or industry) is assumed to be producing shipments, which can be met from current output, P_t, or past production held in inventories, I_t. It is further assumed that the price of output is fixed in each time period and that demand for shipments cannot be transferred from the current period to any subsequent time period. Clearly, if the cost of holding inventories is positive and S_t is known in advance, then $P_t = S_t$ and $I_t = 0$ when factor adjustment is instantaneous. However, when we introduce uncertainty in S_t and lagged adjustment of input factors, it can be shown that cost-minimizing production of shipments may involve $I_t > 0$ and that the cost-minimizing factor production between K and L will depend, ceteris paribus, upon the cost of holding inventories. This model, however, is not consistent with the price of factor services and rate of return on investment embodied in our analysis of the effect of growth of the capital stock on labor productivity. For the present, we adopt the theoretically imperfect position of including inventories as part of the capital stock.

9. In this section, we are following Gollop and Jorgenson (1980).

10. Gollop and Jorgenson also distinguish between the corporate and noncorporate sectors. Their capital stock measures are based on investment series for equipment and plant from 1925 and 1890, respectively, developed by Jack Faucett Associates (1973), with considerable industry and asset detail. Their inventory and land data are based on sources similar to ours.

11. We expect to examine this problem in subsequent work. In particular, we hope to achieve greater asset detail and to disaggregate the manufacturing sector to its durable and nondurable components. Within the framework of the GNP accounts, it is not possible to achieve the industry detail that characterizes Faucett's capital stock estimates.

12. Clark, on the other hand, uses a measure of labor input adjusted for changes in the age-sex composition of the labor force as the denominator of his labor/productivity ratio. The labor input measure in the capital/labor ratio is additionally adjusted for changes in capacity utilization, as noted above. We believe it is clearer for both descriptive and inferential purposes to separate these effects as in our analysis in Table 7.4.

13. A clear explanation and example of the use of this framework appears in Christensen, Cummings, and Jorgenson (1980).

14. Denison also makes adjustment for increasing returns to scale and cyclical movement. However, his adjustment for changes in labor force composition is based on the assumptions outlined above.

15. For these purposes, we have considered shifts only among ten major divisions of the nonfarm business sector: mining, manufacturing, finance, insurance and real estate, construction, transportation, communications, utilities, wholesale and retail trade, and services. A more complete treatment of the effects of labor force composition is found in Gollop and Jorgenson, where six demographic and economic dimensions are employed: age, sex, education, occupation, class of worker (self-employed or employee), and industry. We have not incorporated these results into our analysis because there are some incompatibilities in the respective treatments of data. Denison (1974) argues that occupation and industry are not properly considered part of labor force composition—that is, supply phenomena—but rather are determined by the demand for labor. In our view, this is an open issue with respect to occupation, whose effect is confounded in measurement by the strong association between education and occupation in the Gollop-Jorgenson data. We are inclined at present to agree that the interindustry dimension of labor force composition—like that of capital composition—represents resource allocation, because it results from the pattern of final demand. The translog aggregation of labor inputs is then found by aggregating the growth rates of hours of labor input in each sector, $\dot{L}_i$, weighted by the sector share, c_i, in total labor compensation for the nonfarm business sector. Thus,

$$\dot{L} = \sum_i c_i \dot{L}_i,$$

where

$$\sum_i c_i = 1.$$

16. For strict conformance to our argument in note 15, we should separate the interindustry shifts in the capital stock from the asset effect. However, the former is quite small (because our industry detail is so coarse); therefore, for simplicity in presentation, we have not separated the effects.

17. By way of contrast, Clark (1978, p. 13) obtains a much larger weight relating growth in the capital/labor ratio to growth in labor productivity: .483 or .399, as opposed to capi-

tal's share, which is about .32. The standard errors associated with his estimates of the parameter do not permit one to reject the hypothesis that the true value is equal to capital's share, .2. Further, the annual rate of technical progress embodied in equipment and structures that is implied by Clark's estimate is 100 to 160 percent—implausibly high.

18.   However, as noted above, the measures for the 1973-1977 period are not comparable for cyclical, as well as measurement, reasons.

19.   A clear discussion and explanation of separability and the translog function are given by Denny and Fuss (1977).

20.   The property of functional separability is developed by Berndt and Christensen (1973). The equivalence of this parameter restriction to the imposition of separability is shown in Jorgenson and Lau (1974).

21.   Kmenta and Gilbert (1968) have shown that parameter estimates by the iterative Zellner method are identical to maximum likelihood estimates.

22.   This econometric test is used by Jorgenson and Lau (1974).

23.   This is a test of nested hypotheses. We wish to reject strong separability if there is less than a 5 percent chance that the observed results would occur given strong separability. Since weak separability is a necessary precondition, we must first accept it before the test for strong separability is meaningful. Therefore, we split our chance of rejecting strong separability, when it really exists, between the two tests in an arbitrary fashion.

REFERENCES

Berndt, E. R., and L. R. Christensen, 1973, "The Internal Structure of Functional Relationships: Separability, Substitution, and Aggregation," *Review of Economic Studies* (July):403-10.

Berndt, E. R., and D. O. Wood, 1975, "Technology, Prices, and the Derived Demand for Energy," *Review of Economics and Statistics* (August):259-78.

Christensen, L. R., D. Cummings, and D. W. Jorgenson, 1980, "An International Comparison of Growth in Productivity, 1947-1973," in Kendrick and Vaccara, eds. (1980).

Christensen, L. R., and D. W. Jorgenson, 1970, "The Measurement of U.S. Real Capital Input, 1929-1967," *Review of Income and Wealth* (March):19-50.

Clark, Peter K., 1977, "A New Estimate of Potential GNP," in U.S. Congress, *The Economic Report of the President,* Hearings before the Joint Economic Committee, Part I, pp. 39-54.

_____, 1978, "Capital Formation and the Recent Productivity Slowdown," *Journal of Finance* (June).

Council of Economic Advisers, 1978, *The Economic Report of the President, 1978,* Washington, D.C.: U.S. Government Printing Office, pp. 140-48.

Council on Wage and Price Stability (CWPS), 1978, *A Special Report on Inflation,* Washington, D.C.: U.S. Government Printing Office, pp. 48-58.

Cremeans, J. E., 1974, "Capital Expenditures by Business for Air and Water Pollution Abatement, 1973 and Planned 1974," *Survey of Current Business* (July):58-64.

_____, 1977, "Conceptual and Statistical Issues in Developing Environmental Measures—Recent U.S. Experience," *Review of Income and Wealth* (June):97-115.

Denison, E. F., 1974, *Accounting for U.S. Economic Growth, 1929–1969,* Washington, D.C.: Brookings.

_____, 1978, "Effects of Selected Changes in the Institutional and Human Environment upon Output per Unit of Input," *Survey of Current Business* (January):58–69.

Denny, M., and M. Fuss, 1977, "The Use of Approximation Analysis to Test for Separability and the Existence of Consistent Aggregates," *American Economic Review* (June):404–18.

Gollop, F.M., and D.W. Jorgenson, 1980, "U.S. Productivity Growth by Industry," in Kendrick and Vaccara, eds. (1980).

Hudson, E.A., and D.W. Jorgenson, 1978a, "Energy Prices and the U.S. Economy, 1972–1976," *Data Resources U.S. Review* (September):I.24–I.37.

_____, 1978b, "The Long Term Interindustry Transactions Model: A Simulation Model for Energy and Economic Analysis," report to the Applied Economics Division, Federal Preparedness Agency, General Services Administration, September.

Jack Faucett Associates, 1973, *Development of Capital Stock Series by Industry Sector,* Washington, D.C.: Office of Emergency Preparedness, March.

Jorgenson, D.W., and Z. Griliches, 1967, "The Explanation of Productivity Change," *Review of Economic Studies* (July):249–83.

Jorgenson, D. W., and L. J. Lau, 1974, "Production in the Inter-Industry Model," unpublished memorandum, July.

Kendrick, J. W., 1973, *Postwar Productivity Trends in the United States 1948–1969,* New York: National Bureau of Economic Research.

_____, 1976, *The National Wealth of the United States by Major Sector and Industry,* New York: Conference Board, March.

Kendrick, J. W., and B. N. Vaccara, eds., 1980, *New Developments in Productivity Measurement,* National Bureau of Economic Research, Studies in Income and Wealth, vol. 41, Chicago: University of Chicago Press.

Kmenta, J., and Gilbert, R. F., 1968, "Small Sample Properties of Seemingly Unrelated Regressions," *Journal of the American Statistical Association* (December):180–200.

Mohr, M. F., 1980, "The Long Term Structure of Production, Factor Demand and Factor Productivity in U.S. Manufacturing Industries," in Kendrick and Vaccara, eds. (1980).

Nadiri, M. I., and S. Rosen, 1973, *A Disequilibrium Model of Demand for Factors of Production,* New York: National Bureau of Economic Research.

Norsworthy, J. R., and L. J. Fulco, 1974, "Productivity and Costs in the Private Economy, 1973," *Monthly Labor Review* (June):3–9.

Tornqvist, Leo, 1936, "The Bank of Finland's Consumption Price Index," *Bank of Finland Monthly Bulletin* 10:1–8.

Vaccara, B., 1975, *A Study of Fixed Capital Requirements of the U.S. Business Economy, 1971–1980,* Washington, D.C.: Bureau of Economic Analysis, December.

8 IMPORTED INTERMEDIATE INPUT: *Its Impact on Sectoral Productivity in U.S. Manufacturing*

Frank M. Gollop and Mark J. Roberts

8.1. INTRODUCTION

The energy crisis beginning in 1973, the subsequent production bottlenecks resulting from the shortage of critical raw materials, and persistent inflation have contributed much to the renewed interest in productivity, in general, and sectoral productivity, in particular. These events have made economists increasingly aware of both the interdependence among producing sectors and the dependence of domestic producers on import markets. Of particular concern are those sectors that rely heavily on import markets for intermediate inputs. Given that trade is an important determinant of *economic* growth, trade and trade policy may well be important determinants of *pro-*

The sectoral data and model of factor augmentation developed for this paper are adaptations of the data and sectoral models of production developed by Gollop and Jorgenson (see Gollop, 1974; Gollop and Jorgenson, 1979, 1980). The development of the model of intermediate input reported in this paper is partly based upon research supported by the U.S. Department of Commerce under contract 4025-8188-21141. Any opinions, findings, or conclusions expressed in this paper are those of the authors and do not necessarily reflect the views of the Department of Commerce. We wish to thank John Kaler for many helpful discussions. Any errors or omissions remain the responsibility of the authors.

ductivity growth. The ultimate objective of this paper is to isolate the contributions of imported intermediate input to productivity growth in U.S. manufacturing.

The model developed for this research is based on the sectoral model of production and technical change introduced by Gollop and Jorgenson (1980). They begin with a production function for each industrial sector, giving output as a function of intermediate input, capital input, labor input, and time. Though the Gollop-Jorgenson model is not formally a closed economy model, it does not distinguish between foreign-supplied and domestically produced intermediate inputs. A fundamental objective of this research is to explicitly introduce imported intermediate input as a distinct input into an open economy model of sectoral production. The basic model is developed in section 8.2.

This model provides a useful framework for the measurement of both technical change and the contributions of input growth to *economic* growth, but it cannot isolate the contribution of individual inputs to *productivity* growth. In section 8.3, we restructure the model so that technical change is factor augmenting.[1] We characterize sectoral technology in terms of a factor minimal cost function that is dual to a factor augmentation model of production. Augmentation coefficients associated with input prices become the basis for the evaluation of the unique contributions of distinct inputs to technical change.

We use this cost function to analyze productivity growth in each of twenty-one manufacturing sectors. We develop sectoral data on output and inputs, distinguishing among labor, capital, and foreign-supplied and domestically produced intermediate inputs. Our econometric model is developed in section 8.4. The sectoral data is described in section 8.5.

Our principal objective is to evaluate the direct and indirect contributions of imports and import policy to sectoral technical change. Direct contributions flow directly through inputs; indirect contributions are defined as price effects. If technical change is factor augmenting, inputs serve as mediums of technical change. Estimated augmentation coefficients reveal the input sources contributing directly to productivity growth. Of particular interest is the *direct* contribution associated with imported inputs. In addition, an indirect or price effect may be associated with each input. By affecting prices, trade policy can affect each sector's least-cost combination of inputs and, consequently, the rate of technical change. Tariffs influence the optimal mix of sectoral inputs; quotas similarly limit input choice. Since our model of production does not constrain substitution possibilities, these indirect effects can be identified. Each sector's parameter estimates are used to evaluate the impact of import price changes on productivity growth. Our estimates of direct and indirect effects in each manufacturing sector are reported in section 8.6.

8.2. SECTORAL PRODUCTION AND TECHNICAL CHANGE

An analysis of the structure and sources of technical change must begin with a microeconomic model of production treating all primary and intermediate inputs symmetrically. The traditional macroeconomic orientation of productivity research viewing real value added as output and excluding intermediate input is an overly restrictive characterization of sectoral production.[2] The factors to be considered in a sectoral production account are clearly specified by microeconomic theory. Given a set of market prices, a firm chooses a particular combination of capital, labor, *and* intermediate inputs and presumably alters the composition of that mix in response to changing factor prices. In addition, advances in knowledge (i.e., technical change) may differentially augment individual inputs, thus affecting how the firm reacts to changes in relative factor prices. As a general model, microeconomic theory requires a model of sectoral production with no restrictions on either the particular form of technical change or the marginal rates of substitution among the arguments of the production function.

This general model of sectoral production and technical change can be represented by a production function F for each producing sector:[3]

$$Q = F(M, K, L, I, T),\tag{8.1}$$

where output (Q) is a function of domestically produced intermediate input (M), capital (K), labor (L), imported intermediate input (I), and time (T). We assume that the technology exhibits constant returns to scale and that product and factor markets are competitive.

Logarithmically differentiating the sectoral production function (8.1) with respect to time decomposes the rate of growth of sectoral output into its source components:

$$\frac{d\ln Q}{dT} = \left[\frac{\partial \ln Q}{\partial \ln M} \cdot \frac{d\ln M}{dT} + \frac{\partial \ln Q}{\partial \ln K} \cdot \frac{d\ln K}{dT} \right.$$
$$\left. + \frac{\partial \ln Q}{\partial \ln L} \cdot \frac{d\ln L}{dT} + \frac{\partial \ln Q}{\partial \ln I} \cdot \frac{d\ln I}{dT} \right] + \frac{\partial \ln Q}{\partial T}.\tag{8.2}$$

The rate of growth of the sector's output equals an output elasticity weighted average of the rates of growth of each input plus the rate of technical change. The rate of productivity growth (v_T) is therefore defined as the rate of growth of output holding all inputs constant:

$$v_T \equiv \frac{\partial \ln Q}{\partial T} (M, K, L, I, T). \tag{8.3}$$

Given competitive markets and producer equilibrium, each output elasticity in (8.2) equals the corresponding input's value share:

$$\frac{\partial \ln Q}{\partial \ln X_i} = \frac{p_i X_i}{P_Q Q} \equiv v_i, \tag{8.4}$$

for $i = M, K, L, I$, where the p_i are input prices and P_Q is the price of output. The sectoral rate of technical change can then be written as

$$v_T = \frac{d \ln Q}{dT} - v_M \frac{d \ln M}{dT} - v_K \frac{d \ln K}{dT} - v_L \frac{d \ln L}{dT} - v_I \frac{d \ln I}{dT}, \tag{8.5}$$

where, under constant returns to scale, the value shares sum to unity. The index v_T is a Divisia quantity index of the rate of technical change.[4]

The factor minimal cost function dual to the production function F expresses average cost (C) of sectoral output as a function G of input prices and time:[5]

$$C = G(p_M, p_K, p_L, p_I, T). \tag{8.6}$$

The total rate of growth of average cost can be expressed as the cost elasticity weighted average of rates of growth of input prices plus the rate of change in cost due to technical change:

$$\frac{d \ln C}{dT} = \left[\frac{\partial \ln C}{\partial \ln p_M} \cdot \frac{d \ln p_M}{dT} + \frac{\partial \ln C}{\partial \ln p_K} \cdot \frac{d \ln p_K}{dT} \right.$$
$$\left. + \frac{\partial \ln C}{\partial \ln p_L} \cdot \frac{d \ln p_L}{dT} + \frac{\partial \ln C}{\partial \ln p_I} \cdot \frac{d \ln p_I}{dT} \right] + \frac{\partial \ln C}{\partial T}, \tag{8.7}$$

where, applying Shephard's lemma,[6] each elasticity of average cost with respect to an input price equals that input's share (v_i) in total cost:

$$\frac{\partial \ln C}{\partial \ln p_i} = \frac{p_i X_i}{CQ} = v_i, \tag{8.8}$$

for $i = M, K, L, I$. Consequently, the rate of technical change (v_T) is defined as the negative of the rate of growth of the average cost of sectoral output with respect to time, holding all input prices constant:

$$v_T = -\frac{\partial \ln C}{\partial T} (p_M, p_K, p_L, p_I, T)$$
$$= \left[v_M \frac{d \ln p_M}{dT} + v_K \frac{d \ln p_K}{dT} + v_L \frac{d \ln p_L}{dT} + v_I \frac{d \ln p_I}{dT} \right] - \frac{d \ln C}{dT}. \tag{8.9}$$

The continuous models of production and average cost developed above are useful in incorporating technical change into a model of sectoral production. The dual model of sectoral cost forms the theoretical foundation for this paper. Application of the model to annual data, however, requires that we extend the methodology to incorporate price and quantity data at discrete points in time. We begin by considering the translog cost function,[7] a second-order approximation to the cost function G:

$$C = \exp[\alpha_0 + \sum_i \beta_i \ln p_i + \beta_T T + \frac{1}{2} \sum_i \sum_j \gamma_{ij} \ln p_i \ln p_j$$
$$+ \sum_i \gamma_{iT} \ln p_i \cdot T + \frac{1}{2} \gamma_{TT} T^2]. \tag{8.10}$$

To correspond to a well-behaved production function, the cost function (8.10) must be linear homogeneous in factor prices; that is, a proportional increase in all input prices must increase average cost by the same proportion. This condition is satisfied for the translog cost function at all observations if and only if

$$\sum_i \beta_i = 1,$$
$$\sum_i \gamma_{ij} = 0,$$
$$\sum_i \gamma_{iT} = 0, \tag{8.11}$$

for $i, j = M, K, L, I$.

Taking the logarithmic partial derivatives of (8.10) with respect to each input price and applying (8.8), the behavioral equations that express the firms' demand for inputs take the form

$$v_M = \beta_M + \gamma_{MM} \ln p_M + \gamma_{MK} \ln p_K + \gamma_{ML} \ln p_L + \gamma_{MI} \ln p_I + \gamma_{MT} \cdot T,$$
$$v_K = \beta_K + \gamma_{MK} \ln p_M + \gamma_{KK} \ln p_K + \gamma_{KL} \ln p_L + \gamma_{KI} \ln p_I + \gamma_{KT} \cdot T,$$
$$v_L = \beta_L + \gamma_{ML} \ln p_M + \gamma_{KL} \ln p_K + \gamma_{LL} \ln p_L + \gamma_{LI} \ln p_I + \gamma_{LT} \cdot T,$$
$$v_I = \beta_I + \gamma_{MI} \ln p_M + \gamma_{KI} \ln p_K + \gamma_{LI} \ln p_L + \gamma_{II} \ln p_I + \gamma_{IT} \cdot T. \tag{8.12}$$

The logarithmic partial derivative with respect to time provides an expression for the rate of technical change:

$$-v_T = \beta_T + \gamma_{MT} \ln p_M + \gamma_{KT} \ln p_K + \gamma_{LT} \ln p_L$$
$$+ \gamma_{IT} \ln p_I + \gamma_{TT} \cdot T. \tag{8.13}$$

The parameters γ_{MT}, γ_{KT}, γ_{LT}, and γ_{IT} represent the indirect productivity contribution or price effect associated with individual inputs.

Modeling the rate of technical change in terms of discrete data begins with considering the translog cost function at two points in time, say T and $T - 1$. The average rate of technical change, $\bar{v}_T$, can be expressed as a weighted average of the difference between successive logarithms of input prices minus the difference between successive logarithms of average cost:

$$\bar{v}_T = \sum_i \bar{v}_i[\ln p_i(T) - \ln p_i(T-1)] - [\ln C(T) - \ln C(T-1)], \qquad (8.14)$$

where

$$\bar{v}_T = \frac{1}{2}[v_T(T) + v_T(T-1)],$$

$$\bar{v}_i = \frac{1}{2}[v_i(T) + v_i(T-1)],$$

for $i = M, K, L, I$. The index $\bar{v}_T$ is a Tornqvist index (Tornqvist, 1936) of the rate of technical change.[8] It is a discrete approximation to the continuous index defined in (8.9). Given (8.13), $\bar{v}_T$ can be expressed in terms of the parameters of the translog cost function:

$$-\bar{v}_T = \beta_T + \gamma_{MT}\left[\frac{\ln p_M(T) + \ln p_M(T-1)}{2}\right]$$
$$+ \gamma_{KT}\left[\frac{\ln p_K(T) + \ln p_K(T-1)}{2}\right]$$
$$+ \gamma_{LT}\left[\frac{\ln p_L(T) + \ln p_L(T-1)}{2}\right]$$
$$+ \gamma_{IT}\left[\frac{\ln p_I(T) + \ln p_I(T-1)}{2}\right]$$
$$+ \gamma_{TT}\left[\frac{T + (T-1)}{2}\right]. \qquad (8.15)$$

The behavioral equations (8.12), the time derivative (8.13), and the Tornqvist index of the rate of technical change, $\bar{v}_T$, form the basis for both the factor augmentation model of technical change described in section 8.3 and the econometric model derived in section 8.4.

8.3. FACTOR AUGMENTATION

The basic objective of this section is to restructure the general model of sectoral technical change described in section 8.2 in terms of a model maintaining factor augmentation. The two models differ only in their characterization of technical change. In the general model, the production function shifts over time in response to technical change. In the augmentation model, technical change does not shift the production function; it augments individual inputs. Given a particular restriction on the form of this augmentation, the rate of sectoral productivity growth can be decomposed into components that can be uniquely associated with each input. This model, adapted from a model developed by Gollop and Jorgenson (Gollop, 1974), forms the basis for our empirical evaluation of the direct effects of imported intermediate input on sectoral productivity growth.

Under factor augmentation, each sectoral production function is specified as a function of inputs measured in constant efficiency units, E_i:[9]

$$Q = J(E_M, E_K, E_L, E_I). \tag{8.16}$$

The efficiency units of each factor are equal to the product of the input level and a factor-specific augmentation coefficient, A_i:

$$E_i = X_i \cdot A_i(T), \tag{8.17}$$

for $i = M, K, L, I$, where A_i is a function of time. The production function (8.16) can be rewritten as

$$Q = J [A_M(T) \cdot M, A_K(T) \cdot K, A_L(T) \cdot L, A_I(T) \cdot I]. \tag{8.18}$$

The factor minimal cost function dual to the production function J can be expressed in terms of efficiency unit prices. Since the ith input has price p_i and since it comprises $A_i(T)$ efficiency units, the price of the ith efficiency unit is $p_i/A_i(T)$. Letting $R_i \equiv p_i/A_i(T)$, the sectoral cost function is

$$C = H [R_M(T), R_K(T), R_L(T), R_I(T)]; \tag{8.19}$$

the translog approximation is

$$C = \exp[\alpha_0 + \sum_i \beta_i \ln R_i + \frac{1}{2} \sum_i \sum_j \gamma_{ij} \ln R_i \ln R_j]. \tag{8.20}$$

Stated in terms of input prices and augmentation coefficients, (8.19) and (8.20) become, respectively,

$$C = H \left[\frac{p_M}{A_M(T)}, \frac{p_K}{A_K(T)}, \frac{p_L}{A_L(T)}, \frac{p_I}{A_I(T)} \right] \tag{8.21}$$

and

$$C = \exp\{\alpha_0 + \sum_i \beta_i[\ln p_i - \ln A_i(T)]$$
$$+ \frac{1}{2} \sum_i \sum_j \gamma_{ij}[\ln p_j - \ln A_j(T)][\ln p_i - \ln A_i(T)]\}. \tag{8.22}$$

Applying (8.22) to annual data requires a discrete approximation for each $A_i(T)$. We assume each augmentation coefficient is a translog function of time:[10]

$$A_i(T) = \exp[\eta_i T + \frac{1}{2} \phi_i T^2],\tag{8.23}$$

for $i = M, K, L, I$. Substituting (8.23) into (8.22) results in an estimable approximation to the factor-augmented cost function:[11]

$$C = \exp[\alpha_0 + \sum_i \beta_i \ln p_i - \sum_i \beta_i \eta_i T$$
$$+ \frac{1}{2} \sum_i \sum_j \gamma_{ij} \ln p_i \ln p_j - \frac{1}{2} \sum_i \sum_j \gamma_{ij} \eta_i \ln p_j \cdot T + \frac{1}{2} \gamma_{TT} \cdot T^2],\tag{8.24}$$

where, recognizing that the ϕ_i cannot be identified,

$$\gamma_{TT} = -\sum_i \beta_i \phi_i + \sum_i \sum_j \gamma_{ij} \eta_i \eta_j.\tag{8.25}$$

The complete model of sectoral production includes the cost function (8.24) and the set of conditional factor demand equations. The behavioral equations corresponding to (8.24) are formed by taking the logarithmic partial derivative of the factor-augmented cost function with respect to each efficiency unit price:

$$v_M = \beta_M + \gamma_{MM} \ln p_M + \gamma_{MK} \ln p_K + \gamma_{ML} \ln p_L + \gamma_{MI} \ln p_I$$
$$- (\gamma_{MM}\eta_M + \gamma_{MK}\eta_K + \gamma_{ML}\eta_L + \gamma_{MI}\eta_I) \cdot T,$$
$$v_K = \beta_K + \gamma_{MK} \ln p_M + \gamma_{KK} \ln p_K + \gamma_{KL} \ln p_L + \gamma_{KI} \ln p_I$$
$$- (\gamma_{MK}\eta_M + \gamma_{KK}\eta_K + \gamma_{KL}\eta_L + \gamma_{KI}\eta_I) \cdot T,$$
$$v_L = \beta_L + \gamma_{ML} \ln p_M + \gamma_{KL} \ln p_K + \gamma_{LL} \ln p_L + \gamma_{LI} \ln p_I$$
$$- (\gamma_{ML}\eta_M + \gamma_{KL}\eta_K + \gamma_{LL}\eta_L + \gamma_{LI}\eta_I) \cdot T,$$
$$v_I = \beta_I + \gamma_{MI} \ln p_M + \gamma_{KI} \ln p_K + \gamma_{LI} \ln p_L + \gamma_{II} \ln p_I$$
$$- (\gamma_{MI}\eta_M + \gamma_{KI}\eta_K + \gamma_{LI}\eta_L + \gamma_{II}\eta_I) \cdot T.\tag{8.26}$$

The logarithmic partial derivative with respect to time is

$$-v_T = - (\beta_M\eta_M + \beta_K\eta_K + \beta_L\eta_L + \beta_I\eta_I)$$
$$- (\gamma_{MM}\eta_M + \gamma_{MK}\eta_K + \gamma_{ML}\eta_L + \gamma_{MI}\eta_I) \cdot \ln p_M$$
$$- (\gamma_{MK}\eta_M + \gamma_{KK}\eta_K + \gamma_{KL}\eta_L + \gamma_{KI}\eta_I) \cdot \ln p_K$$
$$- (\gamma_{ML}\eta_M + \gamma_{KL}\eta_K + \gamma_{LL}\eta_L + \gamma_{LI}\eta_I) \cdot \ln p_L$$
$$- (\gamma_{MI}\eta_M + \gamma_{KI}\eta_K + \gamma_{LI}\eta_L + \gamma_{II}\eta_I) \cdot \ln p_I$$
$$+ \gamma_{TT} \cdot T.\tag{8.27}$$

As before, certain restrictions on the factor augmentation model are required to ensure that the cost function is linear homogeneous at each observation:

$$\sum_i \beta_i = 1,$$

$$\sum_i \gamma_{ij} = 0, \tag{8.28}$$

for $i,j = M, K, L, I$. It is important to stress, however, that there are no restrictions on the augmentation coefficients η_i and ϕ_i, for $i = M, K, L, I$.

As it presently stands, the factor augmentation model cannot be used to allocate the rate of productivity growth among its input sources. This decomposition first requires identifying the four augmentation coefficients A_M, A_K, A_L, and A_I. Unfortunately, the four second-order parameters ϕ_M, ϕ_K, ϕ_L, and ϕ_I defining the augmentation functions cannot be econometrically identified. They appear only as part of a nonlinear combination of parameters defining the identified parameter γ_{TT} in (8.25). Consequently, identifying the individual augmentation coefficients requires that factor augmentation be of the first-order exponential form

$$A_i(T) = e^{\eta_i T}, \tag{8.29}$$

for $i = M, K, L, I$, so that $\ln A_i = \eta_i T$. Only then is each augmentation coefficient, A_i, identified. If η_i equals zero, the augmentation coefficient, $A_i(T)$, equals unity. It follows that technical change does not augment the ith input. If η_i is positive (negative), $A_i(T)$ is greater (less) than unity; factor-augmenting technical change increases (decreases) the efficiency units of the ith input. Augmentation of the ith input is a positive (negative) source of economic growth.

Respecifying the factor augmentation model (8.24) in terms of (8.29) leads to the single restriction

$$\gamma_{TT} = \sum_i \sum_j \gamma_{ij} \eta_i \eta_j. \tag{8.30}$$

We refer to (8.30) as the first-order factor augmentation restriction.

Given this particular structure of technical change, the rate of productivity growth can be allocated among its source components. The structure of this decomposition is based on the logarithmic partial derivative of (8.21) with respect to time:

$$\frac{\partial \ln C}{\partial T} = \sum_i \frac{\partial \ln C}{\partial \ln A_i} \cdot \frac{\partial \ln A_i}{\partial T}; \tag{8.31}$$

the rate of change in cost due to technical change equals a cost elasticity weighted sum of the time derivatives of the augmentation functions. Taking the logarithmic derivative of (8.24) with respect to time produces an analogous expression in terms of the translog parameters:

$$
\frac{\partial \ln C}{\partial T} = - \sum_i \beta_i \eta_i - \sum_i \gamma_{Mi} \eta_i \ln p_M - \sum_i \gamma_{Ki} \eta_i \ln p_K
$$
$$
- \sum_i \gamma_{Li} \eta_i \ln p_L - \sum_i \gamma_{Ii} \eta_i \ln p_I
$$
$$
+ [\eta_M \sum_i \gamma_{Mi} \eta_i + \eta_K \sum_i \gamma_{Ki} \eta_i + \eta_L \sum_i \gamma_{Li} \eta_i
$$
$$
+ \eta_I \sum_i \gamma_{Ii} \eta_i] \cdot T. \tag{8.32}
$$

By rearranging terms in (8.32), the change in cost due to technical change can be decomposed into direct contributions associated with each input. The direct contribution through labor input can be expressed as

$$
-\eta_L [\beta_L + \gamma_{ML} \ln p_M + \gamma_{KL} \ln p_K + \gamma_{LL} \ln p_L + \gamma_{LI} \ln p_I
$$
$$
- (\gamma_{ML} \eta_M + \gamma_{KL} \eta_K + \gamma_{LL} \eta_L + \gamma_{LI} \eta_I) \cdot T]. \tag{8.33}
$$

The direct contributions through capital input and domestic and imported materials are defined symmetrically. The sum of the four expressions equals $\partial \ln C / \partial T$ in (8.32).

By specifying the translog cost model in its first-order factor-augmented form, we can isolate the direct contribution of technical change through each input. The critical parameters are η_M, η_K, η_L, and η_I. Referencing equations (8.26) makes clear that the bracketed expression in (8.33) is always positive. Consequently, the sign associated with each direct effect is determined by the sign of the corresponding η_i. If η_i equals zero, the corresponding input does not serve as a medium of technical change. Technical change makes no direct contribution to productivity growth through that input. If η_i is positive, then technical change augments the ith input and thereby makes a direct contribution to the rate of productivity growth. If η_i is negative, the change in technology has reduced the ith input's efficiency content. Retardation of the input reduces productivity growth. These direct contributions are estimated in section 8.6.

8.4. ESTIMATING MODEL

The general model of sectoral technical change described in section 8.2 forms the basis for estimating the indirect productivity effects of input price changes. Evaluating the direct productivity contribution associated with each input requires estimating the factor augmentation model presented in section 8.3. The following description of our econometric model is developed in terms of the augmentation model. However, our discussion applies to the general model as well. Both general and augmentation models have identical error structures. (In this section, when variables such as ϵ are denoted with a single subscript, they represent a vector of observations; when denoted with two subscripts, they represent a particular observation.)

Constructing our estimating model begins with adding random disturbances (ϵ_i) to the four behavioral equations (8.26) and the partial time derivative (8.27):

$$
\begin{aligned}
v_M =\ & \beta_M + \gamma_{MM}\ \ln p_M + \gamma_{MK}\ \ln p_K + \gamma_{ML}\ \ln p_L + \gamma_{MI}\ \ln p_I \\
& - (\gamma_{MM}\eta_M + \gamma_{MK}\eta_K + \gamma_{ML}\eta_L + \gamma_{MI}\eta_I) \cdot T + \epsilon_M, \\
v_K =\ & \beta_K + \gamma_{MK}\ \ln p_M + \gamma_{KK}\ \ln p_K + \gamma_{KL}\ \ln p_L + \gamma_{KI}\ \ln p_I \\
& - (\gamma_{MK}\eta_M + \gamma_{KK}\eta_K + \gamma_{KL}\eta_L + \gamma_{KI}\eta_I) \cdot T + \epsilon_K, \\
v_L =\ & \beta_L + \gamma_{ML}\ \ln p_M + \gamma_{KL}\ \ln p_K + \gamma_{LL}\ \ln p_L + \gamma_{LI}\ \ln p_I \\
& - (\gamma_{ML}\eta_M + \gamma_{KL}\eta_K + \gamma_{LL}\eta_L + \gamma_{LI}\eta_I) \cdot T + \epsilon_L, \\
v_I =\ & \beta_I + \gamma_{MI}\ \ln p_M + \gamma_{KI}\ \ln p_K + \gamma_{LI}\ \ln p_L + \gamma_{II}\ \ln p_I \\
& - (\gamma_{MI}\eta_M + \gamma_{KI}\eta_K + \gamma_{LI}\eta_L + \gamma_{II}\eta_I) \cdot T + \epsilon_I, \\
-v_T =\ & - (\beta_M\eta_M + \beta_K\eta_K + \beta_L\eta_L + \beta_I\eta_I) \\
& - (\gamma_{MM}\eta_M + \gamma_{MK}\eta_K + \gamma_{ML}\eta_L + \gamma_{MI}\eta_I) \cdot \ln p_M \\
& - (\gamma_{MK}\eta_M + \gamma_{KK}\eta_K + \gamma_{KL}\eta_L + \gamma_{KI}\eta_I) \cdot \ln p_K \\
& - (\gamma_{ML}\eta_M + \gamma_{KL}\eta_K + \gamma_{LL}\eta_L + \gamma_{LI}\eta_I) \cdot \ln p_L \\
& - (\gamma_{MI}\eta_M + \gamma_{KI}\eta_K + \gamma_{LI}\eta_L + \gamma_{II}\eta_I) \cdot \ln p_I \\
& + \gamma_{TT} \cdot T + \epsilon_T.
\end{aligned}
\tag{8.34}
$$

Since the value shares v_M, v_K, v_L, and v_I sum to unity, the unknown parameters satisfy the restrictions identified in (8.28), and the disturbances corresponding to the four shares sum to zero: $\epsilon_M + \epsilon_K + \epsilon_L + \epsilon_I = 0$. These four disturbances are not distributed independently.

We assume that the random disturbances for all five equations for the jth observation have expected value equal to zero and a variance-covariance matrix Σ:

$$
E\begin{pmatrix} \epsilon_{Mj} \\ \epsilon_{Kj} \\ \epsilon_{Lj} \\ \epsilon_{Ij} \\ \epsilon_{Tj} \end{pmatrix} = 0, \qquad
\mathrm{var}\begin{pmatrix} \epsilon_{Mj} \\ \epsilon_{Kj} \\ \epsilon_{Lj} \\ \epsilon_{Ij} \\ \epsilon_{Tj} \end{pmatrix} = \Sigma,
$$

for $j = 1, \ldots, N$, where N equals the number of observations for each equation. We also assume that the random disturbances corresponding to distinct observations in the same or distinct equations are uncorrelated. The variance-covariance matrix for the vector of disturbances thus takes the Kronecker product form

$$\text{var} \begin{pmatrix} \epsilon_M \\ \epsilon_K \\ \epsilon_L \\ \epsilon_I \\ \epsilon_T \end{pmatrix} = \Sigma \otimes I_N.$$

While the value shares v_M, v_K, v_L, and v_I in (8.34) can be observed directly from price and quantity data, the rate of technical change v_T is not directly observable. Consequently, we use the Tornqvist index number of the average rate of technical change $\bar{v}_T$ derived at the conclusion of section 8.2:

$$\bar{v}_T = \sum_i \bar{v}_i [\ln p_i(T) - \ln p_i(T-1)] - [\ln C(T) - \ln C(T-1)].$$

Since

$$\bar{v}_i = \frac{1}{2} [v_i(T) + v_i(T-1)],$$

for $i = M, K, L, I$, and

$$\bar{v}_T = \frac{1}{2} [v_T(T) + v_T(T-1)],$$

the estimating equations (8.34) can be written in the form

$$\begin{aligned}
\bar{v}_M &= \beta_M + \gamma_{MM} \overline{\ln p_M} + \gamma_{MK} \overline{\ln p_K} + \gamma_{ML} \overline{\ln p_L} + \gamma_{MI} \overline{\ln p_I} \\
&\quad - (\gamma_{MM}\eta_M + \gamma_{MK}\eta_K + \gamma_{ML}\eta_L + \gamma_{MI}\eta_I) \cdot \bar{T} + \bar{\epsilon}_M, \\
\bar{v}_K &= \beta_K + \gamma_{MK} \overline{\ln p_M} + \gamma_{KK} \overline{\ln p_K} + \gamma_{KL} \overline{\ln p_L} + \gamma_{KI} \overline{\ln p_I} \\
&\quad - (\gamma_{MK}\eta_M + \gamma_{KK}\eta_K + \gamma_{KL}\eta_L + \gamma_{KI}\eta_I) \cdot \bar{T} + \bar{\epsilon}_K, \\
\bar{v}_L &= \beta_L + \gamma_{ML} \overline{\ln p_M} + \gamma_{KL} \overline{\ln p_K} + \gamma_{LL} \overline{\ln p_L} + \gamma_{LI} \overline{\ln p_I} \\
&\quad - (\gamma_{ML}\eta_M + \gamma_{KL}\eta_K + \gamma_{LL}\eta_L + \gamma_{LI}\eta_I) \cdot \bar{T} + \bar{\epsilon}_L, \\
\bar{v}_I &= \beta_I + \gamma_{MI} \overline{\ln p_M} + \gamma_{KI} \overline{\ln p_K} + \gamma_{LI} \overline{\ln p_L} + \gamma_{II} \overline{\ln p_I} \\
&\quad - (\gamma_{MI}\eta_M + \gamma_{KI}\eta_K + \gamma_{LI}\eta_L + \gamma_{II}\eta_I) \cdot \bar{T} + \bar{\epsilon}_I, \\
-\bar{v}_T &= - (\beta_M\eta_M + \beta_K\eta_K + \beta_L\eta_L + \beta_I\eta_I) \\
&\quad - (\gamma_{MM}\eta_M + \gamma_{MK}\eta_K + \gamma_{ML}\eta_L + \gamma_{MI}\eta_I) \cdot \overline{\ln p_M} \\
&\quad - (\gamma_{MK}\eta_M + \gamma_{KK}\eta_K + \gamma_{KL}\eta_L + \gamma_{KI}\eta_I) \cdot \overline{\ln p_K} \\
&\quad - (\gamma_{ML}\eta_M + \gamma_{KL}\eta_K + \gamma_{LL}\eta_L + \gamma_{LI}\eta_I) \cdot \overline{\ln p_L} \\
&\quad - (\gamma_{MI}\eta_M + \gamma_{KI}\eta_K + \gamma_{LI}\eta_L + \gamma_{II}\eta_I) \cdot \overline{\ln p_I} \\
&\quad + \gamma_{TT} \cdot \bar{T} + \bar{\epsilon}_T,
\end{aligned} \tag{8.35}$$

where the average values of each input price and time in the two periods are given by

$$\overline{\ln p_M} = \frac{1}{2} [\ln p_M(T) + \ln p_M(T - 1)],$$

$$\overline{\ln p_K} = \frac{1}{2} [\ln p_K(T) + \ln p_K(T - 1)],$$

$$\overline{\ln p_L} = \frac{1}{2} [\ln p_L(T) + \ln p_L(T - 1)],$$

$$\overline{\ln p_I} = \frac{1}{2} [\ln p_I(T) + \ln p_I(T - 1)],$$

$$\overline{T} = \frac{1}{2} [T + (T - 1)] = T - \frac{1}{2},$$

and each $\overline{\epsilon}_i$ is the average disturbance in the two periods:

$$\overline{\epsilon}_i(T) = \frac{1}{2} [\epsilon_i(T) + \epsilon_i(T - 1)],$$

for $i = M, K, L, I, T$. Note that the average disturbances still sum to zero:

$$\overline{\epsilon}_M + \overline{\epsilon}_K + \overline{\epsilon}_L + \overline{\epsilon}_I = 0;$$

one of the average share equation disturbances depends on the remaining three.

It necessarily follows that the variance-covariance matrix of average disturbances in the ith estimating equations is

$$\text{var}\,(\overline{\epsilon}_i) = \sigma_{ii} \begin{bmatrix} \frac{1}{2} & \frac{1}{4} & 0 \ldots 0 \\ \frac{1}{4} & \frac{1}{2} & \frac{1}{4} \ldots 0 \\ 0 & \frac{1}{4} & \frac{1}{2} \ldots 0 \\ \cdot & \cdot & \cdot \quad \cdot \\ \cdot & \cdot & \cdot \quad \cdot \\ \cdot & \cdot & \cdot \quad \cdot \\ 0 & 0 & 0 \ldots \frac{1}{2} \end{bmatrix}$$

$$= \sigma_{ii}\Omega$$

for $i = M, K, L, I, T$, where Ω is a Laurent matrix. Similarly, the covariance between the ith and jth equations can be written as $\sigma_{ij}\Omega$.[12]

This occurs because the error terms $\bar{\epsilon}_i$, for $i = M, K, L, I, T$, in the transformed specification are no longer uncorrelated over time. The error terms in two adjacent periods, say T and $T - 1$, are both functions of $\epsilon_i(T - 1)$:

$$\bar{\epsilon}_i(T) = \frac{1}{2} [\epsilon_i(T) + \epsilon_i(T - 1)],$$

$$\bar{\epsilon}_i(T - 1) = \frac{1}{2} [\epsilon_i(T - 1) + \epsilon_i(T - 2)].$$

The Laurent matrix describes the pattern of serial correlation among adjacent error terms:

$$V[\bar{\epsilon}_i(T)] = V\left\{ \frac{1}{2} [\epsilon_i(T) + \epsilon_i(T - 1)] \right\}$$

$$= (\frac{1}{2})^2 \{V[\epsilon_i(T)] + V[\epsilon_i(T - 1)] + 2\mathrm{cov}[\epsilon_i(T), \ \epsilon_i(T - 1)]\}$$

$$= \frac{1}{4} [\sigma_{ii} + \sigma_{ii}] = \frac{1}{2} \sigma_{ii},$$

$$\mathrm{cov}[\bar{\epsilon}_i(T), \bar{\epsilon}_i(T - 1)] = \mathrm{cov}\left\{ \frac{1}{2} [\epsilon_i(T) + \epsilon_i(T - 1)], \frac{1}{2} [\epsilon_i(T - 1) + \epsilon_i(T - 2)] \right\}$$

$$= \frac{1}{4} \{\mathrm{cov}[\epsilon_i(T), \ \epsilon_i(T - 1)] + \mathrm{cov}[\epsilon_i(T), \ \epsilon_i(T - 2)]$$

$$+ \mathrm{cov}[\epsilon_i(T - 1), \ \epsilon_i(T - 1)]$$

$$+ \mathrm{cov}[\epsilon_i(T - 1), \ \epsilon_i(T - 2)]\}$$

$$= \frac{1}{4} \sigma_{ii}.$$

Similarly, $\mathrm{cov}[\bar{\epsilon}_i(T), \bar{\epsilon}_i(T - 2)] = 0$.

Since the form of the covariance matrix of average disturbances is the same for each equation (as is the pattern of cross-equation correlation), the variance-covariance matrix for the estimating system has the Kronecker product form

$$\mathrm{var}\begin{pmatrix} \bar{\epsilon}_M \\ \bar{\epsilon}_K \\ \bar{\epsilon}_L \\ \bar{\epsilon}_I \\ \bar{\epsilon}_T \end{pmatrix} = \Sigma \otimes \Omega.$$

Although disturbances in equations for the average value shares and the average rate of technical change are autocorrelated, the data can be transformed to eliminate the autocorrelation. Using a procedure outlined by

Gollop and Jorgenson (1979), we transform the system's data so that the co-variance matrix of transformed disturbances has the required form $\Sigma \otimes I$.

We jointly estimate the $\bar{v}_M$, $\bar{v}_K$, $\bar{v}_L$, $\bar{v}_I$, and $-\bar{v}_T$ equations as a multivariate regression system using a modification of Zellner's method (Zellner, 1962) for seemingly unrelated regressions. At the first stage, all five equations (8.35) are estimated with the restrictions (8.28) imposed. The residuals are used to estimate Σ. Since the resulting estimated Σ will be singular, one of the four share equations is deleted before the second stage. We estimate the parameters of the deleted equation from the linear homogeneity restrictions (8.28). The complete model involves fourteen unknown parameters; five additional parameters can be estimated as functions of the fourteen directly estimated parameters. This method provides estimates that are invariant to the choice of the equation to be dropped.

Having estimated the complete econometric model of factor-augmenting technical change for *each* manufacturing sector, the single first-order factor augmentation restriction (8.30) will be tested for each producing sector. We evaluate this hypothesis by calculating the change in the weighted sum of squared residuals caused by imposing the restrictions relative to the weighted sum of squared residuals of the unrestricted model. When this is multiplied by the residual degrees of freedom (m) divided by the number of restrictions (q), the resulting statistic is distributed as $F(q, m)$. If this hypothesis cannot be rejected, factor augmentation has a first-order form. More importantly, we can use the parameter estimates to determine the magnitude and significance of the direct contributions of augmented imported materials to sectoral productivity growth. The indirect effects of input price changes can be determined directly from the estimates describing the general model of technical change. Our results are reported in section 8.6.

8.5.   DATA BASE

The model of sectoral production introduced in section 8.2 specifies output as a function of time and units of *aggregate* domestic materials, capital, labor, and imported intermediate inputs. Growth accounting requires that each aggregate input be measured in quality-adjusted units. The growth in real labor input between two points in time, for example, may not equal the observed growth in the unweighted sum of hours worked. The composition of the labor force may have changed; that is, the quality of the stock of labor input may have increased or decreased. Measuring the growth in labor input requires accounting for these compositional shifts.

Constructing quality-adjusted measures for each input begins with modeling each aggregate input as a function of individual inputs:

$$
\begin{aligned}
M &= M(M_1, M_2, \ldots, M_n), \\
K &= K(K_1, K_2, \ldots, K_r), \\
L &= L(L_1, L_2, \ldots, L_h), \\
I &= I(I_1, I_2, \ldots, I_q).
\end{aligned}
\tag{8.36}
$$

We assume that each function is homogeneous of degree one in the component inputs.

The rate of growth of each aggregate input can be expressed as an elasticity weighted average of the rates of growth of its components:

$$
\begin{aligned}
\frac{d\ln M}{dT} &= \sum_{m=1}^{n} \frac{\partial \ln M}{\partial \ln M_m} \cdot \frac{d\ln M_m}{dT}, \\
\frac{d\ln K}{dT} &= \sum_{k=1}^{r} \frac{\partial \ln K}{\partial \ln K_k} \cdot \frac{d\ln K_k}{dT}, \\
\frac{d\ln L}{dT} &= \sum_{l=1}^{h} \frac{\partial \ln L}{\partial \ln L_l} \cdot \frac{d\ln L_l}{dT}, \\
\frac{d\ln I}{dT} &= \sum_{j=1}^{q} \frac{\partial \ln I}{\partial \ln I_j} \cdot \frac{d\ln I_j}{dT}.
\end{aligned}
\tag{8.37}
$$

This formulation makes clear that each input's marginal product is the critical characteristic distinguishing input classes within each aggregate function. If the marginal products of all component inputs are equal, there is no theoretical requirement to consider the disaggregate components of each aggregate input.

Under constant returns to scale and competitive markets, the elasticity weights in (8.37) can be replaced with value shares:

$$
\begin{aligned}
\frac{d\ln M}{dT} &= \sum_{m=1}^{n} v_m \frac{d\ln M_m}{dT}, \\
\frac{d\ln K}{dT} &= \sum_{k=1}^{r} v_k \frac{d\ln K_k}{dT}, \\
\frac{d\ln L}{dT} &= \sum_{l=1}^{h} v_l \frac{d\ln L_l}{dT}, \\
\frac{d\ln I}{dT} &= \sum_{j=1}^{q} v_j \frac{d\ln I_j}{dT},
\end{aligned}
\tag{8.38}
$$

where each share weight equals the component input's share in the value of the corresponding input aggregate. In this formulation, differing input prices identify distinct input categories. The aggregates M, K, L, and I are Divisia quantity indexes of sectoral domestic materials, capital, labor, and imported intermediate input, respectively. Prices corresponding to each aggregate input are formed by dividing total expenditures for each aggregate input by the corresponding input index. These prices meet the requirements of proper growth accounting. Each measures the price *per quality-adjusted unit* of the corresponding input.

A set of arguments parallel to those developed in sections 8.2 and 8.3 leads to expressions for each aggregate input in terms of data at discrete points in time:

$$\ln M(T) - \ln M(T-1) = \sum_{m=1}^{n} \bar{v}_m [\ln M_m(T) - \ln M_m(T-1)],$$

$$\ln K(T) - \ln K(T-1) = \sum_{k=1}^{r} \bar{v}_k [\ln K_k(T) - \ln K_k(T-1)],$$

$$\ln L(T) - \ln L(T-1) = \sum_{l=1}^{h} \bar{v}_l [\ln L_l(T) - \ln L_l(T-1)],$$

$$\ln I(T) - \ln I(T-1) = \sum_{j=1}^{q} \bar{v}_j [\ln I_j(T) - \ln I_j(T-1)], \tag{8.39}$$

where the weights $\bar{v}_m$, $\bar{v}_k$, $\bar{v}_l$, and $\bar{v}_j$ equal average value shares of the individual inputs in the total payments made to the corresponding input aggregate. The resulting input aggregates M, K, L, and I are Tornqvist indexes of the sectoral inputs.[13]

We apply the expressions in (8.39) to construct indexes for the aggregate inputs in each sector. Prices per quality-adjusted unit of each input are formed by dividing total expenditures for each input by the corresponding Tornqvist input index. These quality-corrected prices become the aggregate input prices referenced in the cost functions analyzed in sections 8.2 and 8.3.

The construction of aggregate price and quantity indexes for each sector's inputs and of the index number for each sector's average rate of technical change ($\bar{v}_T$) requires detailed price and quantity data for each sector's output and individual inputs. The development of the data must be consistent with the underlying sectoral model of production. First, each aggregate input index must be constructed from data disaggregated by those critical characteristics identifying distinct input classes. Second, since a factor's price is viewed as a measure of the input's marginal value product to producers, all input prices must be measured as producers' prices. Third, to maintain comparability across inputs, across sectors, and over time, a uniform set of control totals must be adopted.

The data constructed by Gollop and Jorgenson (1980) meet all these requirements. They construct measures of labor input, capital services, intermediate input, and output in current and constant prices for forty-five sectors in the private domestic economy. This paper focuses on the subset of industries in the manufacturing group. The twenty-one sectors are listed in Table 8.1.

A complete discussion of the data models is presented in Gollop and Jorgenson (1980). We attempt no exhaustive treatment here. Instead, we provide a brief summary focusing attention on the three theoretical requirements discussed above. First, detailed data matrices for each input are developed. Hours worked by laborers in each sector for each year are cross-classified by sex, age, education, occupation, and employment class of worker. Capital input for each year is disaggregated by industrial sector, type of asset (producers' durable equipment, consumers' durable equipment, residential structures, nonresidential structures, inventories, and land), and legal form of organization (corporate business, noncorporate business, and households and institutions). Constant dollar intermediate in-

Table 8.1.   Manufacturing Sectors

Food and kindred products
Tobacco manufactures
Textile mill products
Apparel and other fabricated textile products
Paper and allied products
Printing, publishing, and allied industries
Chemicals and allied products
Petroleum and coal products
Rubber and miscellaneous plastic products
Leather and leather products
Lumber and wood products, except furniture
Furniture and fixtures
Stone, clay, and glass products
Primary metal industries
Fabricated metal industries
Machinery, except electrical
Electrical machinery, equipment, and supplies
Transportation equipment, except motor vehicles, and ordnance
Motor vehicles and motor vehicle equipment
Professional photographic equipment and watches
Miscellaneous manufacturing industries

put deliveries to each purchasing sector are distinguished by source sectors in each year. Second, all prices are measured in producers' terms. Output is valued net of all indirect business taxes and transportation margins, but gross of all subsidies received by the producing sector. Wages include all supplements paid by employers. The service price of capital is a function of, among other things, income and property taxes, the investment tax credit, and the depreciation structure adopted by the industry. Intermediate input purchases are valued gross of sales and excise taxes and all transportation and trade margins. Third, wherever possible, all component price and quantity data are controlled to national account totals published by the Bureau of Economic Analysis. This preserves the accounting identities inherent in the data and ensures conformity of price and quantity data across inputs, across sectors, and over time.

The sectoral labor, capital, and output data reported in Gollop and Jorgenson (1980) can be used directly in the econometric model developed in section 8.4.[14] However, the econometric model requires that the current and constant dollar intermediate input series be decomposed into domestic and import subsets. While Gollop and Jorgenson estimate total intermediate input in current and constant prices for each sector, they do not distinguish between foreign-supplied and domestically produced intermediate inputs. The point of departure for our model of intermediate input is the Gollop-Jorgenson estimate of total intermediate input in current prices for each manufacturing sector. It equals the difference between output in current prices and value added in current prices. We convert these national accounts estimates to industry boundaries defined according to interindustry (input-output) conventions.

Before describing our particular application of the postwar input-output tables, we find it useful to distinguish between the two distinct categories of imports found in the interindustry transactions matrices. Transferred imports (line 80B) are discussed as follows (U.S. Department of Commerce, 1974, p. 56):

> Imports used for production (i.e., intermediate goods and services) which are substitutable for domestically produced goods and services are treated like secondary products; they are shown as if purchased by the industry producing the substitutable item and added to that industry's output.

A footnote continues:

> Substitutability was determined on a judgmental basis using the following guide: the imports should be interchangeable with a domestically produced item without any changes in the technology of the consuming industry or the resultant product.

Directly allocated imports (line 80A) are discussed as follows:

> Imports used in production which have no domestic counterparts and imports purchased by final users in substantially the same form in which they were imported, are shown as purchased by the consuming industry or final market.

Those imports assigned to line 80A in each private business sector must be treated as imported intermediate input in the production of that sector's output. Those imports assigned to 80B are not intermediate input, but competing products of that sector's domestic product. As such, line 80B imports must not be viewed as part of domestic production. However, as competing output, the imports in 80B find use as intermediate input in those sectors that purchase the product of the corresponding private business sector. Thus, one can view the intermediate input of any business sector as originating from three sources: the imported intermediate inputs directly allocated to line 80A; the domestically produced goods purchased from other business sectors; and the competing intermediate goods imports purchased *through* other business sectors—that is, those goods assigned to line 80B in the sectors supplying intermediate input.

Returning now to the development of the proposed model of intermediate input, we use the input-output coefficients derived from the current price interindustry transactions matrix published for each of the postwar benchmark years to allocate each sector's total intermediate input purchases among all industries supplying that sector. The input-output coefficients are interpolated and extrapolated to obtain shares of intermediate input by sector of origin for each industry for all years. Once the share of intermediate input produced in each source sector has been identified, each source sector's delivery of intermediate input is further allocated to foreign and domestic categories. The bases for allocation are the shares in current prices of imports (line 80B) and domestic production in each source sector's total output. Sectoral output deflators inclusive of indirect business taxes to the supplying sectors are used to convert each source sector's domestically produced output and competing imports to constant prices.[15] The same deflator is applied to domestic production and its competing import since to have been assigned to line 80B, the import is a substitute in use for its domestically produced counterpart. Competitive equilibrium requires an identical market price. Sectoral import price indexes derived from the *Statistical Abstract of the United States* (1950–1976) and "United States Imports for Consumption" (U.S. Department of Commerce, 1947–1973) are used to convert the current price imports directly assigned to line 80A to constant prices. Finally, separate Tornqvist indexes for domestic and foreign-supplied intermediate inputs for each purchasing sector are formed over the appropriate set of constant price intermediate inputs identified for the dis-aggregated source sectors.

It is important to note that the output deflator used in measuring the cur-rent dollar value of a sector's output is not equivalent to the deflator used in evaluating the current dollar value of the sector's output as intermediate in-put into a purchasing sector's production process. The former is measured in producers' prices; the latter is measured in consumers' prices. The former is net of all sales and excise taxes and trade and transportation margins; the latter is gross of sales and excise taxes attributed to the output of the sector supplying the intermediate input. The trade and transportation margins paid by the consuming sector are captured in the intermediate input flows from the trade and transport sectors.

This model of intermediate input preserves the national account totals maintained by Gollop and Jorgenson and, as required by our model of sec-toral production, both distinguishes among unique intermediate inputs de-livered to each sector and measures all input prices in consumers' terms. In addition, the model decomposes intermediate input into its domestic and foreign-supplied subsets. Combined with the sectoral data on output and primary inputs and the econometric model of sectoral production, the inter-mediate input data permit the analysis of the direct and indirect contribu-tions of imported materials to sectoral productivity.

8.6. FINDINGS

Our analysis of the direct and indirect contributions of imported interme-diate input to productivity growth begins with an evaluation of the relative and absolute importance of foreign-produced materials in each U.S. manu-facturing sector. Table 8.2 presents the average cost share of each input over the 1948–1973 period in each of twenty-one manufacturing industries. Relative to other inputs, imported materials account for a small share of production cost in most industries. The average postwar share of imported input ranges from .8 percent in tobacco to 9.2 percent in textiles. The average share across all manufacturing activity is 2.2 percent.[16]

While the imported input cost shares are quite small, the complete time series of factor shares underlying Table 8.2 reveal an important set of de-scriptive statistics. First, the share of foreign-produced materials has been increasing over the postwar period in most industries. The average annual growth rates reported in the last column of the table reveal that imported in-put has become increasingly important in seventeen of twenty-one indus-tries. Second, this is particularly true for the durable goods industries. The

Table 8.2. Average Cost Shares, by Input, 1948–1973

Industry	Labor Input	Capital Input	Average Cost Shares		Average Annual Rate of Growth of Imported Intermediate Input
			Domestic Intermediate Input	Imported Intermediate Input	
Food	.1626	.0614	.7489	.0272	− .0074
Tobacco	.1941	.2718	.5264	.0077	− .0205
Textiles	.2755	.0784	.5544	.0917	.0106
Apparel	.3128	.0357	.6371	.0143	.0143
Paper	.2569	.1374	.5813	.0244	.0041
Printing	.3973	.1052	.4809	.0166	− .0106
Chemicals	.2209	.1755	.5880	.0156	.0057
Petroleum	.1304	.1269	.7047	.0380	.0226
Rubber	.3202	.0966	.5439	.0394	− .0458
Leather	.3365	.0501	.5957	.0176	.0324
Lumber	.3389	.1354	.4987	.0269	.0380
Furniture	.3700	.0729	.5425	.0146	.0267
Stone, clay, and glass	.3431	.1461	.4986	.0121	.0106
Primary metals	.2600	.1186	.5932	.0282	.0192
Fabricated metals	.3478	.0911	.5469	.0141	.0670
Nonelectrical machinery	.3822	.1257	.4821	.0100	.0588
Electrical machinery	.3887	.1010	.4992	.0111	.0419
Transportation equipment	.3744	.0560	.5589	.0108	.0468
Motor vehicles	.2032	.1342	.6504	.0121	.0548
Professional equipment	.4177	.1316	.4402	.0105	.0135
Miscellaneous manufacturing	.3602	.0908	.5209	.0282	.0094

cost shares of imported materials have increased throughout the postwar period in all eleven sectors producing durables. The mean annual rate of growth in this industry group equals 3.5 percent. This compares to 1.5 percent for the six nondurable goods sectors exhibiting increasing import cost shares in the postwar period. Though the sectoral share of foreign-supplied materials in total cost is small in the durables group, the input's relative importance has been increasing at a significant rate over the full postwar period.

The increasing importance of imported materials in manufacturing processes is highlighted further in Table 8.3. The table presents the average annual postwar rates of growth for each input in each manufacturing sector. Each of the underlying input series accounts for the changing composition of individual inputs within each aggregate stock. The rate of growth in foreign-supplied inputs is not only positive in every sector; it is also quite

Table 8.3. Average Annual Rates of Growth of Labor, Capital, Domestic Materials, and Imported Intermediate Input, by Sector, 1948–1973

Industry	Labor Input	Capital Input	Domestic Intermediate Input	Imported Intermediate Input
Food	−.001	.020	.026	.013
Tobacco	−.003	.012	.017	.010
Textiles	−.006	.029	.045	.048
Apparel	.006	.034	.038	.076
Paper	.021	.047	.053	.052
Printing	.017	.008	.048	.037
Chemicals	.026	.042	.065	.069
Petroleum	.001	.019	.044	.063
Rubber	.036	.023	.068	.034
Leather	−.012	.014	.005	.034
Lumber	−.008	.028	.040	.068
Furniture	.016	.029	.055	.080
Stone, clay, and glass	.014	.038	.072	.077
Primary metals	.006	.024	.042	.054
Fabricated metals	.019	.037	.050	.097
Nonelectrical machinery	.020	.047	.060	.116
Electrical machinery	.034	.055	.065	.104
Transportation equipment	.036	.014	.071	.115
Motor vehicles	.016	.034	.058	.110
Professional equipment	.033	.070	.066	.084
Miscellaneous manufacturing	.005	.031	.048	.062

large. It ranges from a low of 1.0 percent in tobacco to 11.6 percent in non-electrical machinery. The average annual rate of growth across all manufacturing industries is 6.7 percent. Consistent with our earlier findings, the postwar rate of growth in imported materials is higher in the durable goods industries than in sectors producing nondurables. The mean rate of growth is 8.8 percent in the former and 4.4 percent in the latter. Moreover, the rate of growth of imported intermediate input exceeds the rate of growth of labor input in all manufacturing sectors except rubber and is larger than the rate of growth of capital input in all but the food and tobacco industries. The rate of growth in imported intermediate input exceeds the growth rates for capital and labor inputs and even the corresponding rate for domestic materials in sixteen of twenty-one sectors. This latter group includes all eleven durable goods industries.

The data presented in Tables 8.2 and 8.3 suggest two conclusions. First, foreign-supplied materials bear a small burden of total industry cost in all but a few sectors, but, second, in terms of both current dollar expenditures and real input levels, imported materials have become an increasingly important part of the production process both in absolute levels and relative to other inputs in nearly all manufacturing sectors. This has been particularly true in *every* durable goods industry. The implication to be derived from the former conclusion is less clear than that to be derived from the latter. The relative unimportance of energy in total manufacturing cost when contrasted with the recent realization of energy's striking importance to the manufacturing process persuades us not to infer that imports have an insignificant effect on manufacturing productivity. In contrast, the implication of imported materials' increasing importance, particularly in sectors that produce durables, is clear. As foreign-supplied inputs increase in absolute and relative importance, we would expect their direct and indirect effects on sectoral productivity growth to increase as well.

8.6.1. Indirect Contributions

Changing input prices affect the least-cost combination of inputs and, consequently, may have *indirect* effects on the rate of technical change. If, for example, technical change is capital-using, an increase in the price of capital not only encourages substitution of other inputs for capital, but also makes the adoption of the capital-using innovation more costly. The result is a lower rate of cost reduction associated with technical change. If, however, technical change is capital-saving, an increase in the price of capital has just the opposite effect on the rate of technical change. Substitution is still encouraged, but now toward an input combination consistent with the capital-saving nature of technical change. Adopting the innovation, by economizing on a now more expensive input, increases the rate of cost reduction associated with productivity growth.[17]

We find it important to emphasize that these potential effects on the rate of technical change are achieved wholly because of changes in prices associated with individual inputs. The input whose price has increased may itself not be a medium of technical change. Its marginal product may not be directly affected by the technical change; that is, its augmentation coefficient may not be a function of time. The sources of productivity growth may well be in other inputs, substitutes, and/or complements. In short, the input may not be a *direct* source of productivity growth; yet it can still have an important *indirect* effect on the rate of technical change. Independent of any direct contribution associated with the input, an increase in its price leads to a new combination of inputs. The indirect effect on technical change is a function of substitution possibilities and the factor-using/factor-saving nature of technical change.

Identifying the direction and magnitude of these indirect effects requires estimating the parameters of the general model of sectoral production and technical change developed in section 8.2. The complete set of estimated coefficients for each sector is reported in Table 8.4. The sectoral parameters of particular interest are γ_{MT}, γ_{KT}, γ_{LT}, and γ_{IT}. Each parameter represents the logarithmic second partial derivative of the translog cost function (8.10) with respect to time and the price of the corresponding input. Equivalently, each represents the logarithmic partial derivative of the rate of cost reduction due to technical change (8.13) with respect to the corresponding input price:

$$\gamma_{iT} = \frac{\partial \left(\dfrac{\partial \ln C}{\partial T} \right)}{\partial \ln p_i} = \frac{\partial(-v_T)}{\partial \ln p_i},$$

for $i = M, K, L, I$. The parameters measure the *indirect* effects associated with the inputs—that is, the effect of an input price change on the rate of cost reduction associated with productivity growth.

The estimates reported in Table 8.4 suggest that technical change is predominantly labor-saving and that domestic materials and imported intermediate are predominantly input-using: γ_{LT} is negative in twenty of twenty-one industries; γ_{MT} and γ_{IT} are positive in eighteen and fifteen sectors, respectively. Increases in the price of labor input almost universally lead to a greater (i.e., more negative) rate of cost reduction associated with technical change; increases in the prices of both domestic and foreign-produced mate-

Table 8.4. Parameter Estimates: Unrestricted Model of Production and Technical Change

Parameters	Food	Tobacco	Textiles	Apparel	Paper	Printing	Chemicals	Petroleum	Rubber	Leather
β_K	.0558[a]	.3486[a]	.0683[a]	.0429[a]	.1119[a]	.1017[a]	.1419[a]	.1255[a]	.0934[a]	.0072[b]
β_L	.1629[a]	.2084[a]	.2662[a]	.3195[a]	.2684[a]	.3945[a]	.2302[a]	.1139[a]	.3378[a]	.3541[a]
β_M	.7577[a]	.4359[a]	.5663[a]	.6209[a]	.5955[a]	.4894[a]	.6115[a]	.7224[a]	.5497[a]	.6134[a]
β_I	.0235[a]	.0070[a]	.0992[a]	.0167[a]	.0242[a]	.0145[a]	.0162[a]	.0382[a]	.0191[a]	.0253[a]
β_T	-.0433	-.0413	-.0460[a]	-.0094	-.0230	-.0075	-.0230	-.0132	-.0205	-.0157
γ_{KK}	.0492[a]	.2054[a]	.0654[a]	.0266[a]	.0796[a]	.0384[a]	.0667[a]	.1189[a]	.0320[a]	.0346[a]
γ_{KM}	-.0270[a]	-.1820[a]	-.0648[a]	-.0156	-.0336[a]	-.0016	-.0060	-.1050[a]	-.0083	-.0357[a]
γ_{KI}	.0013	-.0019	-.0080[a]	.0013	.0024	.0036	.0046[b]	-.0123[a]	-.0074[a]	.0001
γ_{KL}	-.0235[a]	-.0214	.0075	-.0123	-.0484[a]	-.0404[a]	-.0654[a]	-.0016	-.0163[a]	.0010
γ_{KT}	-.0003[b]	-.0012	-.0013[a]	.0004	.0005[b]	-.0002	-.0004	-.0019[a]	-.0004	-.0001
γ_{MM}	.1239[a]	.1928[a]	.2977[a]	.0272	.0248	.0866	-.0102	.5065[a]	.2014[a]	.4679[a]
γ_{MI}	-.0077[b]	.0951[b]	.0702[b]	.0158	.0767[b]	.0514[c]	.0348[c]	-.3159[a]	.0230[c]	.0043
γ_{ML}	-.0891[a]	-.1059[b]	-.3031[a]	-.0274	-.0678[c]	-.1364[c]	-.0186	-.0856[b]	-.2161[a]	-.4365[a]
γ_{MT}	.0032[a]	.0039	.0121[a]	-.0001	.0024[b]	.0041[b]	.0025	.0052[a]	.0081[a]	.0083[a]
γ_{II}	.0041[c]	-.1018[a]	-.0168	-.0136	-.0216	-.0454[b]	-.0116	.2430[a]	.0071[c]	.0149
γ_{IL}	.0023	.0086	-.0454[a]	-.0035	-.0575[a]	-.0097	-.0279[c]	.0852[a]	-.0228[b]	-.0192
γ_{IT}	-.0003[b]	-.0005	.0024[a]	.0002	.0016[a]	-.0001	.0010[b]	-.0018[a]	-.0007[b]	.0010[a]
γ_{LL}	.1103[a]	.1187[a]	.3410[a]	.0432	.1737[a]	.1864[a]	.1120	.0019	.2552[a]	.4546[a]
γ_{LT}	-.0032[a]	-.0022	-.0132[a]	-.0005	-.0046[a]	-.0038[b]	-.0032	-.0015[b]	-.0069[a]	-.0093[a]
γ_{TT}	-.0018	-.0028	-.0017	.0000	-.0015	.0001	.0001	-.0020	-.0000	-.0008

Table 8.4 *continued*

Parameters	Lumber	Furniture	Stone, Clay, and Glass	Primary Metals	Fabricated Metals	Nonelectrical Machinery	Electrical Machinery	Transportation Equipment	Motor Vehicles	Professional Equipment	Miscellaneous Manufacturing
β_K	.1773[a]	.0618[a]	.1262[a]	.0844[a]	.0828[a]	.1116[a]	.1038[a]	.0483[a]	.1397[a]	.1296[a]	.0892[a]
β_L	.3033[a]	.3611[a]	.3192[a]	.2717[a]	.3514[a]	.3629[a]	.3653[a]	.3837[a]	.2018[a]	.3778[a]	.3017[a]
β_M	.4853[a]	.5579[a]	.5412[a]	.6092[a]	.5435[a]	.5087[a]	.5125[a]	.5511[a]	.6407[a]	.4805[a]	.5740[a]
β_I	.0341[a]	.0191[a]	.0133[a]	.0347[a]	.0223[a]	.0169[a]	.0183[a]	.0168[a]	.0178[a]	.0120[a]	.0350[a]
β_T	.0129	-.0165	-.0065	-.0082	-.0101	-.0084	-.0312	-.0039	-.0256	-.0225	-.0185
γ_{KK}	.0902[a]	.0514[a]	.0954[a]	.0522[a]	.0645[a]	.0457[a]	.0470[a]	.0092[b]	.0645[a]	.0100[a]	.0442[a]
γ_{KM}	-.0518[a]	-.0292[a]	.0331	-.0195[c]	-.0390[a]	.0148	.0436[b]	.0127	-.0290[a]	-.0616[a]	.0216
γ_{KI}	.0020	.0017[b]	.0022	.0045	.0037[a]	.0003	-.0019	-.0021[b]	-.0039[a]	-.0076	.0047
γ_{KL}	-.0404[b]	-.0240[a]	-.1307[a]	-.0372[a]	-.0292[a]	-.0608[a]	-.0887[a]	-.0198[b]	-.0316[a]	-.0308[c]	-.0705[a]
γ_{KT}	.0011[c]	-.0002	.0024[b]	-.0006[b]	.0002	.0007[b]	.0016[a]	-.0001	.0005	.0013[b]	.0010
γ_{MM}	-.0933	-.0775	-.0354	-.0030	.3344[a]	.2703[b]	-.1690	.6588[a]	.1009	.9862[a]	.1077
γ_{MI}	.0793[a]	.0026	.0162	.0254	-.0518	-.0619[b]	.2938[a]	.1160	-.0482	-.2999[b]	-.0173
γ_{ML}	.0658	.1041[c]	-.0139	-.0029	-.2436[a]	-.2232[c]	-.1684	-.7874[a]	-.0237	-.6247[a]	-.1120
γ_{MT}	-.0017	-.0013	.0043	.0009	.0053[a]	.0077[a]	.0044[c]	.0199[a]	.0005	.0176[a]	.0068
γ_{II}	-.0926[a]	-.0042	.0060	-.0104	.0436	.0561[b]	-.2545[a]	-.0830	.0619	.2075[b]	.0077
γ_{IL}	.0114	-.0001	-.0243	-.0195	.0045	.0054	-.0374	.0309[c]	-.0098	.0999[c]	.0049
γ_{IT}	.0010[b]	.0004[c]	.0009[c]	.0012[b]	.0006[b]	.0006	.0014[a]	.0012[b]	.0009[c]	-.0020	.0005
γ_{LL}	-.0367	-.0800	.1689	.0595	.2683[a]	.2786[b]	.2945[b]	.8381[a]	.0651	.5557[a]	.1775
γ_{LT}	-.0005	.0011	-.0076	-.0016	-.0061[a]	-.0089[a]	-.0075[a]	-.0210[a]	-.0019	-.0170[a]	-.0084[c]
γ_{TT}	.0015	-.0009	.0000	-.0003	-.0007	-.0005	-.0013	.0002	-.0003	-.0005	-.0003

[a]Significant at the 99 percent level.
[b]Significant at the 95 percent level.
[c]Significant at the 90 percent level.

rials lead to reduced rates of productivity growth in most sectors. Technical change is capital-saving in ten sectors and capital-using in eleven industries.

Of particular interest to this paper are the direction, magnitude, and statistical significance of the indirect effects associated with foreign-supplied inputs. The estimated coefficient γ_{IT} is positive in fifteen manufacturing industries. This group notably includes all but one durable goods sector. The positive parameter estimates are statistically significant at the 95 percent level in nine sectors. Of the six estimates having negative values, only three are statistically significant. The summary conclusion is that in three of four manufacturing industries, technical change is imported intermediate input–using, suggesting that increasing import prices lessen the rate of cost reduction achieved through technical change.

Given that imported materials represent only slightly more than 2 percent of manufacturing cost, we are not surprised to find that the negative indirect effect of imported materials on the rate of technical change is quite small. The statistically significant positive estimates of γ_{IT} range from .001 in chemicals, leather, and lumber to .0024 in textiles. The mean value of γ_{IT} across this set of estimates is .0013, suggesting that, on average, a 10 percent increase in the price of imported materials decreases the rate of technical change (i.e., reduces the rate of cost reduction associated with technical change) by less than two one-hundredths of a percentage point.

The surprising result inferred from Table 8.4, however, is that despite the relatively insignificant cost share of imported materials, the indirect effect associated with foreign-produced inputs is seldom the least among all indirect effects. In particular, the magnitude of γ_{IT} is less than the magnitudes of γ_{KT}, γ_{MT}, and γ_{LT} in only six sectors. The best indication of the relative importance of the imported input-using nature of technical change is derived from a sector-by-sector comparison of γ_{IT} and γ_{KT}. While ex ante impressions might lead one to expect changing capital prices to have larger and more significant productivity effects than changing import prices, the evidence indicates otherwise. Despite the fact that the mean cost share of imported materials is only one-fifth as large as the mean share of capital costs in manufacturing activity, γ_{IT} is larger than γ_{KT} in twelve of twenty-one industries. Moreover, the estimate of γ_{IT} is statistically significant at the 95 percent level in twelve industries, as compared to nine for γ_{KT}. Changes in the prices of foreign-supplied materials are no less important determinants of the sectoral rate of productivity growth than are changes in the prices of capital goods.

The single most important finding regarding the indirect productivity effects of imported inputs is that technical change is imported materials–using in all durable goods industries except professional equipment. Increases in import prices therefore will reduce the rate of technical change in ten of eleven durable goods sectors, and it is precisely this industry group that has experienced a significant average annual increase (3.5 percent per year) in the cost share of foreign-produced inputs and a substantial average annual rate of growth (8.8 percent per year) in the employment of imported inputs. As imported materials become increasingly important in the production of durable goods, the negative impact of rising import prices on the sectoral rates of technical change will increase as well.

8.6.2. Direct Contributions

A model of production incorporating factor-augmenting technical change maintains that productivity growth occurs in ways uniquely related to individual inputs. In particular, inputs become the mediums of technical change. Productivity growth is the result of technical change that augments individual inputs. Factor-specific augmentation coefficients model these effects. Sectoral production becomes a function of augmented input levels.

If factor-augmenting technical change makes no direct contribution to economic growth through a particular input, the augmentation coefficient corresponding to that input will not be a function of time. If technical change makes a positive (negative) contribution through an input, the corresponding augmentation coefficient will be a positive (negative) function of time.

The model of factor-augmenting technical change introduced in section 8.3 is a reparameterized form of the general model of technical change developed in section 8.2. Each augmentation coefficient is initially modeled as a translog function of time. As motivated in section 8.3, the augmentation coefficients cannot be econometrically identified unless augmenting technical change takes the first-order exponential form. This leads to the first-order factor augmentation restriction defined in (8.30). We test this restriction for each sector. The resulting test statistics are reported in Table 8.5. We cannot reject the hypothesis in any sector.

We impose this first-order structure on the augmentation functions and estimate the parameters of each sectoral model of production and technical change. The estimates are reported in Table 8.6. The critical parameters are η_K, η_L, η_M, and η_I. Each represents the rate of change in the corresponding augmentation function with respect to time. While the parameter estimates are seldom statistically significant at conventional levels, they are unbiased estimates of the true production coefficients. Estimates having positive values indicate that technical change augments the corresponding inputs and

Table 8.5. First-Order Factor Augmentation

Industry	F-Test Statistic
Food	.564
Tobacco	.462
Textiles	3.759
Apparel	.000
Paper	.752
Printing	.001
Chemicals	.004
Petroleum	.173
Rubber	.100
Leather	.128
Lumber	.476
Furniture	.204
Stone, clay, and glass	.000
Primary metals	.016
Fabricated metals	.493
Nonelectrical machinery	.407
Electrical machinery	.485
Transportation equipment	.031
Motor vehicles	.002
Professional equipment	.358
Miscellaneous manufacturing	.167

NOTE: The critical value F (1, 86) = 3.96 at the 95 percent level.

consequently makes a direct contribution to the rate of productivity growth through these inputs. Estimates having negative values indicate that the change in technology reduces the efficiency content of the corresponding inputs. The direct contribution of technical change through these inputs retards productivity growth.

While the direction of each contribution is solely a function of the sign of the corresponding η, the magnitude of each contribution is a function of the complete set of parameter estimates and the data. Equations describing the decomposition of the rate of change in cost due to technical change among its source components are derived in section 8.3. The direct contribution associated with each input is defined in (8.33). We apply (8.33) to each sector's data and parameter estimates to measure the impact on average cost of technical change through each augmented input. Negative values imply that augmentation of that input reduces average cost (increases productivity growth); positive values indicate that augmentation of that input leads to increased cost (decreased productivity growth).[18] The decomposition is reported in Table 8.7.

In most instances, factor-augmenting technical change has increased the efficiency content of individual inputs. The result is a reduction in average cost. This is especially true for labor input. The direct cost contribution of technical change flowing through labor input is negative in nineteen of twenty-one industries. The contributions of capital, domestic materials, and imported intermediate input have negative values in thirteen, ten, and ten sectors, respectively. Consistent with ex ante impressions, augmentation of labor and capital inputs contributes to productivity growth in most sectors.

The most interesting finding derived from Table 8.7 is that this conclusion does not apply to the postwar history of imported materials. In eleven of twenty-one industries, augmentation of imported inputs has had a retarding effect on the rate of productivity growth. While technical change has augmented some inputs, it has reduced the efficiency content of imported inputs. Once again, we find that this retarding effect is clustered in the durable goods industries. Seven of the eleven sectors that experienced reduced rates of productivity growth because of the retardation of imported materials lie within the durables group. Among these seven industries, the average annual rate of cost reduction due to technical change is *decreased* by an average .114 tenths of a percentage point because of the retarding impact of imported materials. Depending on the sector being considered, this retarding contribution diminishes the sectoral rate of productivity growth by an amount ranging from 5 to 20 percent.

The estimates reported in Table 8.7 reveal two other important findings. First, we cannot conclude that the augmentation of imported materials makes the least contribution to the rate of technical change in all sectors. In fact, the contribution of technical change through imported intermediate input is larger than the contribution through capital input in eight industries. This result is particularly striking given that the mean share of imported materials in total cost is less than one-fifth of the average cost share of capital input. Second, whether technical change through imported input has had a stimulating or retarding effect on the rate of productivity growth, the contributions in each sector have generally been increasing over the postwar period. The last column of Table 8.7 reports the average annual change in the contribution of augmented foreign materials to sectoral productivity. In sixteen of twenty-one sectors, the contribution (column 4), whether positive or negative, has been increasing (column 5) over the 1948–1973 period. In short, the direct contribution of technical change through augmented foreign-produced materials has become larger over the postwar period.

Table 8.6. Parameter Estimates: First-Order Factor Augmentation Model of Production and Technical Change

Parameters	Food	Tobacco	Textiles	Apparel	Paper	Printing	Chemicals	Petroleum	Rubber	Leather
β_K	.0557[a]	.3479[a]	.0673[a]	.0429[a]	.1117[a]	.1016[a]	.1419[a]	.1255[a]	.0935[a]	.0070[b]
β_L	.1622[a]	.2080[a]	.2648[a]	.3194[a]	.2678[a]	.3942[a]	.2304[a]	.1132[a]	.3376[a]	.3545[a]
β_M	.7583[a]	.4374[a]	.5678[a]	.6210[a]	.5960[a]	.4899[a]	.6111[a]	.7234[a]	.5499[a]	.6130[a]
β_I	.0238[a]	.0067[a]	.1000[a]	.0168[a]	.0244[a]	.0143[a]	.0166[a]	.0379[a]	.0190[a]	.0254[a]
γ_{KK}	.0497[a]	.2069[a]	.0655[a]	.0269[a]	.0796[a]	.0387[a]	.0669[a]	.1185[a]	.0320[a]	.0347[a]
γ_{KM}	-.0271[a]	-.1846[a]	-.0650[a]	-.0160	-.0321[a]	-.0013	-.0065	-.1079[a]	-.0080	-.0354[a]
γ_{KI}	.0005	-.0024	-.0079[a]	.0009	.0000	.0036	.0044[a]	-.0109[a]	-.0074[a]	-.0001
γ_{KL}	-.0232[a]	-.0199	.0075	-.0118	-.0475[a]	-.0409[a]	-.0649[a]	.0003	-.0167[a]	.0008
γ_{MM}	.1243[a]	.2078[a]	.3095[a]	.0243	.0709	.0579	.0348	.5577[a]	.2287[a]	.4840[a]
γ_{MI}	-.0018	.0796[a]	.0591[b]	.0183[a]	.0362	.0464[a]	.0078	-.3074[a]	.0221[c]	-.0049
γ_{ML}	-.0954[a]	-.1028[b]	-.3036[a]	-.0265	-.0749[c]	-.1030	-.0362	-.1424[a]	-.2428[a]	-.4438[a]
γ_{II}	.0029[c]	-.0796[a]	-.0085	-.0136[a]	.0074	-.3553[a]	-.0037	.2105[a]	.0069[c]	.0185[a]
γ_{IL}	-.0016	.0025	-.0426[a]	-.0056	-.0437[a]	-.0145	-.0085	.1079[a]	-.0216[c]	-.0135[a]
γ_{LL}	.1202[a]	.1203[b]	.3387[a]	.0439	.1660[a]	.1584[b]	.1096	.0343	.2811[a]	.4565[a]
η_K	.0222	.0099	.0250[b]	-.0042	.0055	.0298[b]	.0708	.0121	.1359	-.0014
η_L	.0456[b]	.0223	.0472[a]	.0182	.0215	.0214[b]	.0687	-.0571	.0335	.0175
η_M	.0131	.0013	.0042	.0056	-.0029	-.0070	-.0089	-.0077	-.0484	-.0020
η_I	.1011[c]	-.0017	.0389	.0205	-.0210	-.0152	.0155	.0295	.5165	-.0343

180

Table 8.6 *continued*

Parameters	Lumber	Furniture	Stone, Clay, and Glass	Primary Metals	Fabricated Metals	Nonelectrical Machinery	Electrical Machinery	Transportation Equipment	Motor Vehicles	Professional Equipment	Miscellaneous Manufacturing
β_K	.1772[a]	.0618[a]	.1262[a]	.0843[a]	.0827[a]	.1113[a]	.1033[a]	.0482[a]	.1397[a]	.1294[a]	.0901[a]
β_L	.3039[a]	.3609[a]	.3191[a]	.2715[a]	.3521[a]	.3635[a]	.3651[a]	.3841[a]	.2022[a]	.3791[a]	.3007[a]
β_M	.4849[a]	.5582[a]	.5414[a]	.6096[a]	.5429[a]	.5083[a]	.5137[a]	.5472[a]	.6397[a]	.4784[a]	.5741[a]
β_I	.0340[a]	.0192[a]	.0133[a]	.0346[a]	.0223[a]	.0169[a]	.0179[a]	.0205	.0184[a]	.0131[a]	.0350[a]
γ_{KK}	.0900[a]	.0513[a]	.0954[a]	.0525[a]	.0645[a]	.0457[a]	.0471[a]	.0094[a]	.0644[a]	.1004[a]	.0484[a]
γ_{KM}	−.0525[a]	−.0289[b]	.0335	−.0205	−.0393[a]	.0147	.0421[b]	.0261	−.0295[a]	−.0681[a]	.0274
γ_{KI}	.0028	.0017[a]	.0014	.0043[a]	.0040[a]	.0004	−.0005	−.0167	−.0037[a]	−.0043	.0069
γ_{KL}	−.0403[b]	−.0240[a]	−.1303[a]	−.0364[a]	−.0292[a]	−.0607[a]	−.0887[a]	−.0187[b]	−.0312[a]	−.0281	−.0827[b]
γ_{MM}	−.0677	−.0722	−.0271	−.0087	.3459[a]	.2711[b]	−.0445	.9585	.1646[c]	.6557[a]	−.0632
γ_{MI}	.0707[a]	.0059	.0023	.0151	−.0642	−.0595[a]	.1765[a]	−.0983	−.0897[c]	−.1097[c]	−.0178
γ_{ML}	.0496	.0952[c]	−.0087	.0141	−.0242[a]	−.2263[c]	−.1740	−.8863	−.0453	−.4780[b]	.0536
γ_{II}	−.0926[a]	−.0057	.0134[b]	−.0056	.0556	.0539[a]	−.1487[a]	.0311	.0936[c]	.0780	−.0016
γ_{IL}	.0191[b]	−.0018	−.0171	−.0137	.0045	.0052	−.0272[c]	.0839	−.0002	.0360	.0124
γ_{LL}	−.0284	−.0693	.1561	.0361	.2672[a]	.2818[b]	.2899[b]	.8212[a]	.0768	.4701[b]	.0166
η_K	−.0069	.0068	−.0798	.0543	−.0005	.0199	.0314	−.5334	.0216	−.0050	−.0184
η_L	.0047	.0101	−.0275	.0759	.0154	.0203[c]	.0336[c]	.0689	.0465	.0309[b]	.0228
η_M	.0071	.0023	.0524	−.0344	−.0084	−.0203	−.0023	.0187	.0141	−.0011	.0027
η_I	.0143	.0787	−.0875	−.0491	−.0213	−.0353[b]	−.0013	−.3588	.0086	−.0093	.1904

[a] Significant at the 99 percent level.
[b] Significant at the 95 percent level.
[c] Significant at the 90 percent level.

181

Table 8.7. Contributions of Technical Change through Augmented Inputs to the Rate of Change in Sectoral Cost

Industry	Direct Contributions (average annual rate in tenths of 1 percent)				Average Annual Change in Contribution of Imported Intermediate Input
	Labor Input	Capital Input	Domestic Intermediate Input	Imported Intermediate Input	
Food	−.7428	−.1373	−.9799	−.2754	.0024
Tobacco	−.4319	−.2673	−.0687	.0013	−.0000
Textiles	−1.3030	−.1986	−.2322	−.3560	−.0038
Apparel	−.5685	.0150	−.3572	−.0293	−.0004
Paper	−.5517	−.0759	.1684	.0514	.0000
Printing	−.8506	−.3139	.3364	.2219	−.0164
Chemicals	−1.5147	−1.2521	.5225	−.0241	−.0002
Petroleum	.7487	−.1542	.5415	−.1121	−.0017
Rubber	−1.0709	−1.3121	2.6318	−2.0592	.1001
Leather	−.5865	.0071	.1193	.0594	.0021
Lumber	−.1600	.0919	−.3547	−.0383	−.0011
Furniture	−.3740	−.0502	−.1246	−.1136	−.0031
Stone, clay, and glass	.9458	1.1736	−2.6038	.1057	.0009
Primary metals	−1.9706	−.6505	2.0383	.1371	.0028
Fabricated metals	−.4087	.0046	.3909	.0294	.0014
Nonelectrical machinery	−.7771	−.2512	.9770	.0342	.0019
Electrical machinery	−1.3085	−.3170	.1147	.0014	.0001
Transportation equipment	−2.5285	3.0319	−1.0511	.4830	−.0207
Motor vehicles	−.9437	−.2904	−.9175	−.0102	−.0004
Professional equipment	−1.2945	.0658	.0483	.0096	.0002
Miscellaneous manufacturing	−.8258	.1669	−.1401	−.5324	−.0094

182

8.7. CONCLUSION

The important summary conclusion of this research is that foreign-supplied materials and import policy do have important direct and indirect effects on the sectoral rate of productivity growth in U.S. manufacturing. In over three-fourths of the manufacturing sectors and in all but one durable goods industry, increases in import prices have a detrimental impact on the sectoral rates of technical change. This indirect effect is the result of sectoral substitution possibilities and the imported input–using nature of technical change. Moreover, the direct contribution of technical change associated with augmented foreign materials diminishes the rate of cost reduction associated with productivity growth in eleven manufacturing sectors. Once again, the durable goods industries are more than proportionately represented in this group. While the overall magnitudes of these direct contributions and price effects are generally small, they are quite large relative to the very small share of manufacturing cost allocated to imported inputs. In fact, the direct productivity contributions and the price effects associated with foreign-supplied materials exceed the corresponding estimates for capital input in nearly half of the manufacturing sectors.

Given that the cost share of imported materials has risen over the postwar period in all but four sectors and that the average rate of growth in the employment of imported inputs exceeds the growth rate recorded for every other input in over three-fourths of the manufacturing industries, we must infer that the direct contributions and price effects observed in the postwar period will most likely increase in the future. This inference is particularly relevant to the durable goods industries, which together account for nearly 65 percent of manufacturing activity. Imported materials cost shares and real input use have grown most rapidly in these sectors. Moreover, detrimental direct contributions and indirect effects associated with this input are clustered in this industry group. This study clearly identifies the sectors that produce durable goods as the group of manufacturing industries whose productivity is most influenced by imports and that is therefore most sensitive to trade policy.

NOTES

1. The application of factor-augmenting technical change in the context of translog models has been discussed by Gollop (1974), Berndt and Wood (1975), Berndt and Jorgenson (1975), Woodland (1976), Wills (1979), Gollop and Jorgenson (1979), and Gollop and Roberts (1981).

2. A model of sectoral production excluding intermediate input formally maintains value-added separability. The model of production introduced below does not require this restriction.

3. Formally, there is a separate production function F^i for each of n sectors:

$$Q_i = F^i(M_i, K_i, L_i, I_i, T),$$

for $i = 1, 2, \ldots, n$. There is no requirement that the sectoral production functions be identical. To minimize notation, we suppress the industry subscript i in the text.

4. Jorgenson and Griliches (1967) and Christensen and Jorgenson (1969) discuss and apply a form of this index appropriate for an aggregate study of productivity growth.

5. Note that the cost function G maintains constant returns to scale as required by the production function F. Average cost in (8.6) is not a function of output.

6. Shephard's lemma (Shephard, 1953) says that the derivative of the cost function with respect to a factor price equals the conditional factor demand.

7. The translog function was introduced by Christensen, Jorgenson, and Lau (1971, 1973). We maintain that the translog cost function exhibits symmetry, a property required of all well-behaved factor-minimal cost functions. Symmetry implies that the matrix of the function's second partial derivatives is symmetric. Stated in terms of the translog parameters, this requires that $\gamma_{ij} = \gamma_{ji}$ and $\gamma_{iT} = \gamma_{Ti}$, for all i and j.

8. See Gollop and Jorgenson (1980, pp. 11–16).

9. See Dixit (1976, pp. 16–42) for an excellent discussion of augmentation coefficients and efficiency units.

10. Though the translog expansion of $A_i(T)$ formally has an intercept term, it is set equal to zero; that is, $A_i(T)$ is indexed to unity when $T = 0$.

11. Since the translog function is a second-order approximation, all terms involving higher-order expressions are set equal to zero.

12. All variables and error terms in equation system (8.35) are two-period averages. Consequently, the number of observations per equation is reduced from N to $N - 1$. The vector $\bar{\epsilon}_i$ is thus $(N - 1) \times 1$ and the dimension of the Laurent matrix Ω is $(N - 1) \times (N - 1)$.

13. For a complete discussion of the model of sectoral input, see Gollop and Jorgenson (1979, pp. 3–16).

14. It is important to emphasize that the final current and constant price output series developed by Gollop and Jorgenson include all domestic output designed for either domestic or export markets and exclude all secondary products transferred into producing sectors from either domestic or foreign production. The output series therefore measures total domestic production. This is precisely the conceptual measure of output required by our model. We therefore use the Gollop-Jorgenson output series directly.

15. The price indexes are taken from Gollop and Jorgenson (1980).

16. The current dollar cost share of directly allocated imports in *total imported materials* is large in only three of twenty-one manufacturing industries—food products, rubber, and miscellaneous manufacturing. For these three industries, the average cost share is approximately 60 percent. Directly allocated imports in four other industries—chemicals; stone, clay, and glass products; machinery, except electrical; and electrical machinery—have an average cost share equal to approximately 15 percent. All other manufacturing sectors have directly allocated input cost shares less than 8 percent.

17. See Binswanger (1974) for a good discussion of the relationship among biased technical change, changing input prices, and their effects on cost shares and input use.

18. Recall that the rate of change in cost due to technical change equals the negative of the rate of technical change. See equation (8.9). Consequently, *negative* contributions to average cost imply *positive* contributions to the rate of productivity growth.

REFERENCES

Berndt, E. R., and D. W. Jorgenson, 1975, "Energy, Intermediate Goods, and Production in an Inter-Industry Model of the U.S., 1947–1971," paper delivered at the World Congress of the Econometric Society, Toronto.

Berndt, E. R., and D. O. Wood, 1975, "Technical Change, Tax Policy and the Derived Demand for Energy," unpublished manuscript, Department of Economics, University of British Columbia, Vancouver.

Binswanger, H. P., 1974, "The Measurement of Technical Change Biases with Many Factors of Production," *American Economic Review* 64, no. 6:964–76.

Christensen, L. R., and D. W. Jorgenson, 1969, "The Measurement of U.S. Real Capital Input, 1929–1967," *Review of Income and Wealth,* series 15:293–320.

Christensen, L. R., D. W. Jorgenson, and L. J. Lau, 1971, "Conjugate Duality and the Transcendental Logarithmic Production Function," *Econometrica* 39, no. 4: 255–56.

———, 1973, "Transcendental Logarithmic Production Frontiers," *Review of Economics and Statistics* 55, no. 1:28–45.

Cowing, T., and R. Stevenson, eds., 1981, *Productivity Measurement in Regulated Industries,* New York: Academic Press.

Dixit, A. K., 1976, *The Theory of Equilibrium Growth,* London: Oxford University Press.

Gollop, F. M., 1974, "Modeling Technical Change and Market Imperfections: An Econometric Analysis of U.S. Manufacturing, 1947–1973," unpublished Ph.D. dissertation, Harvard University.

Gollop, F. M., and D. W. Jorgenson, 1979, "Sources of Productivity Growth in the Postwar U.S.," unpublished manuscript.

———, 1980, "United States Factor Productivity by Industry, 1947–1973," in Kendrick and Vaccara, eds. (1980).

Gollop, F. M., and M. J. Roberts, 1981, "The Sources of Growth in the U.S. Electric Power Industry," in Cowing and Stevenson, eds. (1981).

Jorgenson, D. W., and Z. Griliches, 1967, "The Explanation of Productivity Change," *Review of Economic Studies* 34, no. 99:31–64.

Kendrick, J. W., and B. N. Vaccara, eds., 1980, *New Developments in Productivity Measurement,* National Bureau of Economic Research, Studies in Income and Wealth, vol. 41, Chicago: University of Chicago Press.

Shephard, R. W., 1953, *Cost and Production Functions,* Princeton, N.J.: Princeton University Press.

Statistical Abstract of the United States, 1950–1976, Washington, D.C.: U.S. Government Printing Office.

Tornqvist, L., 1936, "The Bank of Finland's Consumption Price Index," *Bank of Finland Monthly Bulletin* 10:1–8.

U.S. Department of Commerce, 1947–1973, "United States Imports for Consumption," Washington, D.C.: U.S. Government Printing Office.

U.S. Department of Commerce, Interindustry Economics Division, 1974, "The Input-Output Structure of the U.S. Economy: 1967," *Survey of Current Business* 54, no. 2:24–56.

Wills, J., 1979, "Technical Change in the U.S. Primary Metals Industry," *Journal of Econometrics* 10, no. 1:85–98.

Woodland, A. D., 1976, "Modelling the Production Sector of an Economy: A Selective Survey and Analysis," Department of Economics Discussion Paper 76-21, University of British Columbia, Vancouver.

Zellner, A., 1962, "An Efficient Method of Estimating Seemingly Unrelated Regressions and Tests for Aggregation Bias," *Journal of the American Statistical Association* 57, no. 298:348–68.

NAME INDEX